INDUCTION TO TRAGEDY

INDUCTION TO TRAGEDY

A STUDY IN A DEVELOPMENT OF FORM IN *GORBODUC, THE SPANISH TRAGEDY* AND *TITUS ANDRONICUS*

HOWARD BAKER

NEW YORK
RUSSELL & RUSSELL · INC

REISSUED, 1965, BY RUSSELL & RUSSELL, INC.
BY ARRANGEMENT WITH LOUISIANA STATE UNIVERSITY PRESS
L. C. CATALOG CARD NO: 65-17875

To Mary Anderson Hill

Printed in the United States of America

NOTE

THIS STUDY is the result of intermittent work during the past ten years. It has been much befriended. Professors W. D. Briggs and H. D. Gray of Stanford University gave impetus to its beginnings; Professor Emile Legouis of the Sorbonne helped to bring it through its clumsy middle stages; later at the University of California, Professor Willard Farnham, whose own studies had been running parallel with this one, was generous in giving both encouragement and information, and when the study finally became a dissertation for the Ph.D., Professor Farnham and Professors George Potter, James M. Cline, and Bertrand H. Bronson lent aid so materially and with such good will that the task of producing a formal document was far from onerous; and very recently when the study had to be reconsidered from the point of view of publication, Professor F. O. Matthiessen of Harvard University furnished both detailed and general suggestions which greatly simplified the problems of revision. Certain pages in Chapter II and in Chapter III appeared originally in *Modern Language Notes* and in *Modern Philology;* the right to reprint them is gratefully acknowledged.

HOWARD BAKER

CONTENTS

INTRODUCTION

TO DESCRIBE in historical terms some of the formal elements in that art which we call Elizabethan tragedy is the general objective of this book. I expect, and am prepared to respect, an immediate denial that Elizabethan tragedy has a form definite enough to support generalization. But we do talk about "Elizabethan tragedy," and when we do so we must have, whatever our reservations may be, some fairly definite form in mind. How definite it is at the beginning of Shakespeare's career, or how definite it ought to be in our minds, where it came from, what were the processes of its development—these are our main problems.

Tragic form, I take it, can be looked at from two important angles—from the angle of craftsmanship or technique and from the angle of ethical or moral significance. Technique, in turn, can be divided up into a number of lesser masteries, such as for instance the masteries over the medium of expression, over plot, over construction, and over character. Moral significance, in its turn, though it is scarcely reducible to a variety of simpler terms, at least can be detected on various levels of simplicity and complexity, ranging from out-and-out sensationalism or pure didacticism up to tragic attitudes that cannot easily be confined to formula. And, generally speaking, the more difficult the materials mastered, both technical and moral, the greater is the artistic victory.[1] * The primary intention of this study is to show in some detail how Elizabethan tragedy, without changing importantly the kind of technical and moral material which it had inherited from the Middle Ages, and without being influenced centrally by Seneca, moved fairly smoothly through victories over more and more difficult and significant versions of those materials.

Hence the articulation of the ensuing chapters. The problems treated in connection with *Gorboduc*, the subject of Chapter I—the relations to traditional drama, to Seneca, to contemporary politics and morality, to esthetics in general—are simple and foundational. Chapter II, a study of the formation of heroic blank verse, is a deliberate simplification, a review of one special technique; it describes the developing ability to express a more and more complicated subject matter. Chapter III, in examining *The Spanish Tragedy* and *Titus Andronicus* as typical tragedies of blood, and in estimating the theoretic contribution of Seneca, turns to fairly complex structural problems; and Chapter IV describes certain important structural features which the dramatic tragedy adapted from the medieval metrical tragedy. The final chapter pursues the subject of technique over into the field to which it will inevitably fly; it undertakes to consider tragedy on its

* The notes to this book will be found on pp. 221 ff.

most difficult level, to give some account of the ethical form in pre-Shakespearean tragical literature, the principles of which are derived mainly from the data in the earlier chapters.

The limits in time are roughly those indicated by the plays named above. *Gorboduc* makes a good starting point, since its position at the beginning of the great period is clear cut, and since all the problems that bear on it are definite preliminaries to later problems. *Titus Andronicus* would make a good stopping point if it did not seem better sometimes to frame observations so as to include some of the later Shakespearean drama; *Titus Andronicus*, however, is the logical and really the actual end of this study, for I find that I have most to say about the drama which is called Senecan. The last sentence indicates the limits in scope: interested in the principles of tragic form, I have not attempted to give attention to all available examples of early tragedy.

In a way I also am writing about "The Medieval Heritage of Elizabethan Tragedy," and after Professor Willard Farnham's valuable book of that title, as well as after the varied and estimable studies of Lily B. Campbell, Hardin Craig, E. E. Stoll, William Witherle Lawrence, Theodore Spencer, Walter Clyde Curry, and others, there seems to be little occasion to dwell here upon the implications in Professor Curry's excellent axiom: "The seventeenth century and its successors could have exerted no possible influence upon sixteenth century accomplishment." [2] The accomplishment of the later sixteenth century needs must have been built on earlier accomplishment; the magnificent form attained by tragedy could not have been plucked, not even by a Shakespeare, out of the morning air. And however we construe the history of the period, we shall end by agreeing that the stamp of the Middle Ages, be it large or small, rests upon the achievement of the years during which Shakespeare was maturing. That it was a deep and incisive stamp, and one not to be greatly obliterated even by Shakespearean genius, is at least the implication in the findings which I am about to set down.

But since the literary historians who have respected Professor Curry's axiom have tended also to search almost exclusively for influences on the drama in earlier examples of the drama, I should say a word to support another proposition which is basic to all that follows: in the sixteenth century Englishmen did not differentiate sharply between a play designed for production on the stage and a certain kind of "tragical" narrative. Thus the medieval conception that such writers as Lucan wrote tragedies persisted; and as late as 1598 Francis Meres could say, "As Accius, M. Atilius, and Milithus were called *Tragaediographi*, because they writ tragedies: so may wee truly terme Michael Drayton *Tragaediographus* for his passionate penning the downfals of valiant Robert of Normandy, chast Matilda, and great Gaueston."[3] One might note, too, that authors of metrical tragedies frequently employ dramatic terminology: the ghost of "Forrex," in *The Mirror for Magistrates*, for instance, says, "Complayne

I may with *tragiques* on the *stage*."[4] The method of the following chapters is governed, therefore, by the principle that the influences of nondramatic writing are to be considered side by side with those of writing fashioned directly for the stage.

And a word about Seneca. Naturally any study attending so closely as this one to the structure and effect of pre-Shakespearean tragedy must have a good deal to say about Seneca; I have found it necessary to say very much indeed, but it has nearly all gone down on the negative side of the ledger. The theory that Seneca was the eminent influence on sixteenth century writers of tragedy is, I think, a blighting critical fiction. It rests, so far as I can see, on an entirely unjustified extension of the many egregious distortions in John W. Cunliffe's dissertation, *The Influence of Seneca on Elizabethan Tragedy* (London, 1893); therefore I have used this work as the center for my discussion of Seneca in the following chapters. But it must be remarked emphatically that Professor Cunliffe himself drew back from the top-heavy theories which his followers erected upon his research. In the Introduction to his *Early English Classical Tragedies* (Oxford, 1912), he recommends caution again and again; at one place, for instance, in commenting on another scholar's extreme version of his own theories, he writes, ". . . we must not overlook the importance of the native and popular elements which contributed most materially to the vitality of the new form of art and prepared the way for its acceptance on the public stage."[5]

The chapter in *The Cambridge History of English Literature* shows a similar reluctance to let the theoretic Influence of Seneca run too far out of bounds.

As a whole, an un-Senecan view of early Elizabethan tragedy is extremely uncommon. A sentence like this one from Theodore Spencer's illuminating study *Death and Elizabethan Tragedy* has been for me valuable as an exception: ". . . Seneca's effect was chiefly upon dramatic technique, hardly at all upon language, and only a little more upon ideas." [6] With the last two phrases I am in agreement; I shall propose some revision of the opinion in regard to dramatic technique. And another valuable exception, I have found in the work of Willard Farnham: "When Elizabethan tragedy reveals that the same mankind which has capacity for spiritual nobility must live and die in a physical world productive of grossness and horror, it is able to raise in us a tragic qualm such as Seneca, with his shower of horrors upon men and women intrinsically ignoble, can never make us feel."

To conclude this introduction, I shall set down three quotations which may stand as emblems of my particular interests and intentions in this book. The first is Theodore Spencer's interpretation of the sixteenth-century conflict between love of life and scorn of life as the source of the great drama:

On the one hand, the present world, the value of thc individual and his right to fame are considered increasingly important; on the other, man's sin, the vanity of worldly life and the imminence of death are to be contemplated with the greatest possible intensity. . . . A conflict between these two opposing attitudes to life was inevitable, and the result was not only drama in a technical, but also in a deeper, a psychological and sociological, sense.

The second has to do with my interest in the principles of dramatic form; it is Gustav Freytag's statement of his initial assumption:

Even an elaborate system of specific rules, a certain limitation, founded in popular custom, as to choice of material and structure of the piece, have been at different periods the best aid to creative power.[7]

The third is doubly remarkable in that it appeared in a masterpiece of Shakespearean criticism, which, brilliant in its discipline, eschewed all historical aspects of the subject.

A total reverse of fortune, coming unawares upon a man who 'stood in high degree,' happy and apparently secure, —such was the tragic fact to the mediaeval mind. It appealed strongly to common human sympathy and pity; it startled also another feeling, that of fear. It frightened men and awed them. It made them feel that man is blind and helpless, the plaything of an inscrutable power, called by the name of Fortune or some other name,—a power which appears to smile on him for a little, and then on a sudden strikes him down in his pride.[8]

This is A. C. Bradley's description of the root-substance of Shakespearean tragedy. "Shakespeare's idea of the tragic fact," Bradley continues, "is larger than this idea and goes beyond it; but it includes it . . ." If it includes this purely medieval conception of tragedy, this way of seeing tragedy which was founded, as Freytag phrases it, in popular custom, how many more limitations upon material and structure did it inherit? And how is it larger than its inheritance? How does it go beyond it?

CHAPTER I

GORBODUC: SOME FUNDAMENTAL PROBLEMS IN THE EARLY DRAMATIC TRAGEDY

GORBODUC has been more than usually subject to the vicissitudes of opinion. Composed in 1561 by Thomas Sackville and Thomas Norton and played as "furniture of part of the grand Christmasse in the Inner Temple,"[1] it was acted at Queen Elizabeth's invitation, a month later before her in Whitehall Palace. While its style and morality inspired the encomiums of Sir Philip Sidney, its failure to abide rigidly by Aristotle's precepts of regularity drew his condemnation.[2] To Edward Alde it was apparently a political piece, for Alde reprinted it in 1590 as an appendix to Lydgate's *Serpent of Division,* a prose work on the evils of the civil wars in the time of Julius Caesar. During the following century it belonged to oblivion. Then Thomas Rymer, using it as a club to inflict his militant pedantry, described it inaccurately and commended it heartily.[3] And Alexander Pope, in his concern for its "propriety in sentiments, dignity in sentences, and unaffected perspicuity of style," committed himself to the opinion that the tragedy has virtues which "all succeeding poets, not excepting Shakespeare himself, either little understood, or perpetually neglected."[4] With these overtures, *Gorboduc* returned to the polite world, dressed out sumptuously in an edition printed in 1736; and immediately it fell back into oblivion.

Thomas Warton, the younger, made motions towards retrieving it; but, besides arbitrarily amputating one of its authors from it, Warton, in his account, was hampered by an unfortunate metathesis of the name Gorboduc. In transcribing William Griffith's title page Warton twisted *Gorboduc* into *Gordobuc*, and he let the confused form persist throughout his extended discussion of the tragedy. The error is especially curious since another metathesis appears to be historically a part of the development of the name: for Geoffrey of Monmouth King Gorboduc is King Gorbogudo. But the difference between a variant and a blunder is so vast that Joseph Ritson in a single pointed sentence could make Warton's whole chapter look ridiculous.

For modern scholars *Gorboduc*, over and above its chronological significance, makes two special appeals for notice. One group of critics—Schelling, Ward, H. Schmidt, and Cunliffe [5]—sees it as a strictly Senecan tragedy. Another group—L. H. Courtney, L. Toulmin Smith, and S. A. Small [6]—sees it primarily as a political piece which aimed to persuade Elizabeth to resolve the question of the succession to her throne. For the former critics the play is Senecan in form and rhetoric, and, in view of the prominence of blood, of murder and revenge, also Senecan in content: "*Gorboduc* is pure Seneca," says Schelling.[7] For the latter critics the play is essentially native English and political in content, a representation of political division, dissension, and rebellion; rhetorically and even to a certain extent formally it follows, they believe, the molds of political oratory: "The play," says Courtney, "is rather a political argument than a simple tragedy." [8] The fruits of these Senecan and political investigations are collected in Homer Andrew Watt's study of the play.[9] But Professor Watt, aiming at inclusiveness and exhaustiveness, has reconciled only the most glaring of the inconsistencies in the two critical approaches, and so today criticism of *Gorboduc* is in a state of uncomfortable dualism. The old play itself is referred to by all and read by few. The few readers that it wins to itself hold it, either with deference or with condescension to Pope, to be utterly dull and, with sheer indifference to the rules of Sidney and Rymer, regular to the point of being dreary.

The varied and mutually exclusive views of the play must be re-examined. *Gorboduc* is probably not a unified whole, but in certain parts preponderantly literary and in other parts preponderantly political; and these parts are in all likelihood the separate contributions of the two authors. By approaching *Gorboduc* through the problem of division of authorship, I think that a somewhat more just view of the play, and of early Elizabethan tragedy in general, can be obtained.

I.

The question of authorship has been tossed about with even greater abandon than have been the esthetic questions concerning the play itself. For two hundred years Thomas Norton suffered the misfortune of having his collaborator's name descend through the generations of a prominent and estimable family. The mischief began when John Dryden, wishing in his Dedication of *The Rival Ladies* to flatter the Earl of Dorset, referred to the author of *Gorboduc* as "that famous Lord Buckhurst, afterwards Earl of Dorset, and progenitor to that excellent person, who (as he inherits his soul and title) I wish may inherit his good fortune." Perhaps ignorance was responsible for Dryden's rejection of Norton, for Dryden, along with Oldham, was under the persuasion that King Gorboduc was a woman. Nevertheless Norton's name was divorced from the play until Thomas Warton reopened the question.

Warton, however, only made matters worse for Norton. For, at about the time *Gorboduc* was first being played, Thomas Norton had engaged in an unlucky poetical enterprise: he contributed twenty-eight versified Psalms to the metrical Psalter of Sternhold and Hopkins, and these psalms, signed with Norton's initials, had descended through the successive editions of the Book of Common Prayer to smite Warton's finer senses in the course of every service. And so Warton complains:

> . . . if we may judge from [Norton's] share in our metrical psalmody, he seems to have been much more properly qualified to shine in the miserable mediocrity of Sternhold's stanza, and to write spiritual rhymes for the solace

of his illuminated brethern, than to reach the bold and impassioned elevations of tragedy.[10]

These psalms, it is true, are no masterpieces of poetry; they do not, however, justify Warton's chastising a true Presbyterian with the invective that is usually reserved for Methodists. Indeed, Warton's historical perspective has failed him here, for actually the miserably mediocre stanza of Sternhold—fourteener couplets—was not shunned by the translators of the accepted examples of bold and impassioned tragedy in Norton's period—the Senecan tragedies; this despised meter was used, moreover, despite the example of Surrey, by Phaer, the most esteemed of the translators of Virgil. Warton nevertheless is positive in his rejection of Norton; and his critical successors agreed with him so thoroughly that in 1859 R. W. Sackville-West, another member of the family of which Lord Buckhurst was the progenitor, could reprint the play without putting Norton's name on the title page.

But today critics are convinced that Norton's claim to a share in *Gorboduc* is undeniable. The evidence in his favor, as a matter of fact, is unusually abundant. The three editions of the play, in 1565, 1570, and 1590, assign the tragedy to both authors. While the first of these editions was unauthorized and the third was printed from the first,[11] the second was fully authorized; and John Day, the printer of the authorized edition, appears to be as well informed as he is garrulous about the *authors* of *Gorboduc*. No contemporary reference throws the least doubt upon this evidence.

In point of fact Jasper Heywood, in his introduction to *Thyestes* (1560), puts Norton's name beside Sackville's; and Gabriel Harvey, in two separate references to *Gorboduc*, says that it is by Lord Buckhurst and Mr. Norton.[12] Collaboration was common in this period: and the two young men were associated in the Inner Temple and in Elizabeth's first parliaments; as poets, they doubtless saw each other in the house in which Norton lived, that of the puritan printer, Edward Whitchurch, the stepfather of Norton's wife and one of the initiators of *The Mirror for Magistrates*, to which Sackville contributed.

It would be possible even to argue on Warton's own grounds that Thomas Norton has a better claim to a share in *Gorboduc* than has Thomas Sackville. For Warton grounds his case on versification, and the notable fact about the verse of *Gorboduc* is that it is blank verse, the first blank verse, so far as is known both from sixteenth century testimony[13] and from modern research, that was employed in the drama. Before *Gorboduc*, blank verse had been used by the Earl of Surrey in his translation of Books II and IV of the *Aeneid* and by Nicholas Grimald in two contributions to Tottel's *Miscellany;* thus the meter appeared in print for the first time in 1554, and again in 1557. Its next known appearance is contained in the work of the man whom Warton scorned as a metrist;[14] for Thomas Norton in translating Calvin's *Institutes of the Christian Religion*, adopted blank verse in rendering into English two passages which Calvin had quoted from Virgil. Norton's translation was first published on May 6, 1561. Consequently, so far as the evidence shows, it must have been Norton, rather than Sackville, who came to the writing of *Gorboduc* with previous experience in that auspicious medium which the first notable dramatic tragedy inaugurated on the stage.

2.

Although *Gorboduc* is indisputably a product of joint authorship, the evidence that Norton wrote the first three acts and Sackville the last two is insubstantial. These are the divisions which William Griffith, the printer of the surreptitious edition of 1565, assigns to the respective authors. But John Day, in the authorized edition, although he is unusually communicative about the authors, makes no assignments; this may indicate uncertainty on his part. The edition of 1590 merely repeats Griffith in this as in other respects. The value of Griffith's information—that is, of the only information that we have on the matter—is questionable. According to John Day, Griffith obtained a copy of the play from "some young man" who "lacked a litle money and much discretion" when in 1565 Sackville was out of England and Norton far out of London.[15] It is quite possible that a "young man" who possessed a copy of the manuscript may have been able to provide Griffith with fairly reliable information; a flat statement of this kind would seem scarcely to be totally inaccurate. But the one contemporary statement of the relative shares of Norton and Sackville comes from a man whom the authorized printer and apparently the authors themselves took pains to discredit.

Modern critics, in attempting to resolve the problem by studying the text of the play, have been inclined to handicap themselves by looking for distinguishing differences where such differences could not exist. We must argue along with Professor Watt that, in general mechanics, *Gorboduc* had to be all of a piece.[16] There can scarcely be marked differences in the mechanics of versification, for instance, when blank verse, a stiff new meter, is making its first appearance in the drama: such phenomena as variations in the length of line and the introductions of rhyme are most certainly accidental. Similarly there is scarcely room for strong personal variations in the handling of the external form of the classical drama, of that stiff new form of five acts with choruses. The play, besides, must have a certain general uniformity in tone since its political morality, in its larger aspects at least, was the matter of perhaps greatest interest and importance to both authors, as well as the deliberately chosen theme of the whole tragedy. Nor, in view of Norton's previous experiments in blank verse, is there reason for assuming that Sackville possessed enormously superior poetic energies.

Yet I believe that there are distinguishing traits of the separate hands hidden under these broad aspects of uniformity. These will be examined in subsequent sections of this chapter.

There has also been made some effort to identify the parts of the play by tabulating the mannerisms of the respective authors. In this the assumptions are sound: individual peculiarities of diction ought to indicate the individual contributors. But the difficulty is to find genuine mannerisms of one author or the other; so far, I believe, no convincing evidence of this kind has been established. F. Koch, a German scholar, thought, for instance, that the repetition of words—like, "Once, once haue hapt," "Thou, Porrex, thou . . ."—which occurs rather frequently in the last two acts and only once in the first three, was an indication of Sackville's hand; [17] and in this conclusion he is followed by Professor Watt. But repetition of words is not, properly speaking, a mannerism of Sackville; it occurs frequently in Norton's versified psalms.[18] The only other bit of evidence of this kind, in which the critics have shown faith, is the appearance of the word *hugie* in the last two acts of the play and not at all in the first three acts. *Hugie* occurs a half-dozen or so times in Sackville's poetry exclusive of *Gorboduc;* I have not encountered it in Norton's work. But the use of a word like *hugie* is scarcely a mannerism, for the word is an example of sophisticated poetical diction, developed apparently to meet the need for dissyllables in the metrical line, and employed rather commonly by the poets of the sixteenth century. It is the kind of peculiar, catchy, and useful word that would slip readily in and out of a poet's vocabulary. *Hugie* is at once too common and too uncommon to be a good test of authorship.[19]

The final proposition of the scholars who find a difference between the early and late parts of the play is best summed up in the words of Koch:

> In der zweiten Hälfte pulsiert ein viel frischeres dramatisches Leben, als in der ersten und wird dadurch selbstverständlich auch die ganze Diktion beeinflusst, ohne dass man allerdings dieses gerade schematisch nachweisen könnte.[20]

So general a statement requires no discussion here. Later pages in this chapter will show, I think, that it is essentially true.

3.

In political terms *Gorboduc* is a warning against the rebellions and civil wars which follow upon uncertainty in the succession of the crown. The warning is aimed directly at Elizabeth; for in the early years of her reign Englishmen looked on the future with foreboding: Elizabeth was in ill health, the succession was in doubt, her immediate predecessors had had very short reigns, and strife between the extreme protestants and the Catholics smoldered throughout the country. According to the will of Henry VIII, which had been given authority by the Act of Succession, the successor to Elizabeth, if she were to die heirless, would be Lady Katharine Grey. The weight of Katharine Grey's claim to the throne, however, was doubtful. Henry's will had been disputed by Northumberland at the time of Edward's death; and, while Catholics were unwilling even to concede legitimacy to Elizabeth, they would have been totally opposed to granting precedence to Katharine, a descendant of Henry's younger sister, over Mary Stuart, the descendant of his elder sister. But most threatening of all was the fact that Katharine came from a hotly protestant family. Consequently Elizabeth's first parliaments pleaded with her either to establish an appointed successor as firmly as possible—the appointed successor in all probability would have been Katharine Grey—or to marry and produce an heir. *Gorboduc* in effect is saying to Elizabeth: take good advice; resolve the question of the succession, lest uncertainty lead us into "tumults, rebellions, arms, and civil wars." Elizabeth, of course, did nothing, for she was intent on picking her way gingerly between Catholicism and protestantism.

But within this framework of political significance there is room for more than one political philosophy. There are in *Gorboduc*, I think, two distinct philosophies, not wholly contrasting philosophies but ones which, starting from the same position, look in different directions. I shall attempt to state them by paraphrasing certain lines in the text. The one may be put as follows:

When a prince, refusing sage counsel, succumbs to flattery and allows the succession to be broken, civil strife follows. But no subject may call to account the doings of a prince; nor may any subject rebel against a prince in act or in speech or even in secret thought.[21]

The other philosophy may be framed thus:

When a prince, refusing sage counsel, succumbs to flattery and allows the succession to rest in doubt—then, if the prince dies suddenly, civil strife follows. Therefore parliament should convene and should appoint an heir to the throne—a rightful heir by virtue of birth within the native land, and by virtue of descent or of "some former law." [22]

In these two views the common lesson in political morality is that monarchs should harken to good advice and rule wisely; if they do not, they and their nation will be overtaken by ruin. This is the general lesson of the chief metrical tragedies from the work of Lydgate through *The Mirror for Magistrates.* In *The Complaint of the Duke of Buckingham* Sackville himself expresses his devotion to the text for these numerous political sermons:

> Byd kings, bid kesars, bid all states beware . . .
> Who reckles rules, right soone may hap to rue.[23]

Beyond the common ground of general morality, these political doctrines diverge sharply in that the one is unlimitedly monarchical and the other is parliamentary. The first sees, as the fruit of monarchic mistakes, the horror of civil war, and ends in an emotional contemplation of the wickedness of any sort of rebellion. The second, without condoning rebellion, proceeds immediately to ways and means of avoiding monarchic mistakes—that is, to parliamentary action. The first pursues error into unmitigated catastrophe, a course which is not uncongenial to tragedy, as is proved by the medieval metrical tragedies, by the Senecan tragedies, and by the "hugger-mugger" conclusion of *Hamlet.* The second ends in a specific *moralitas:* it applies the fable to the cause of Lady Katharine Grey and to this cause alone.

The first doctrine, that of extreme monarchism, is the core of the first scene of the fifth act of *Gorboduc*. It is expressed most pointedly by Eubulus, the good counsellor, who says:

> Eke fully with the duke my minde agrees
> That no cause serues wherby the subiect maye
> Call to accompt the doynges of the prince,
> Muche lesse in bloode by sworde to worke reuenge,
> No more then maye the hande cut of the heade.
> In acte nor speache, no, not in secrete thoughte,
> The subiect maye rebell against his lorde,
> Or iudge of him that sittes in Caesars seate . . .
>
> (V, 1, 41–8)

Monarchism here is so extreme that an eighteenth-century commentator, after quoting the laudations of Mr. Pope and describing the elegant edition which Mr. Spense had given the play, suggests that "the strongly pointed Antirevolutional principles at the conclusion have had a share" in throwing *Gorboduc* "nearly again into its former state of neglect." This critic then produces as evidence the lines given above.[24]

I am proposing of course that Thomas Sackville was the vigorous monarchist. The monarchism in question can be defined further by examining its counterpart, that is, the value put upon common people, statements of which occur in almost identical words in this scene and in *Buckingham*. Farther along in the speech from which we have just quoted, Eubulus ejaculates:

So giddy are the common peoples mindes,
So glad of chaunge, more wauering than the sea . . .
. . . the rascall routes
. . . Are neuer trustie to the noble race.
(V, 1, 72–3; 100, 102)

And Buckingham complains:

O let no prince put trust in commontie,
Nor hope in fayth of giddy people's mynde,
But let all noble men take heede by mee,
That by the proofe to well the payne do fynde:
Loe, where is truth or trust? or what could bynde
The vayne people, but they will swerue and swaye,
As chaunce brings chaunge, to driue and draw that way? [25]

In flat contradiction to this antithesis, in Act V, Scene 1, of the sacred prince with the giddy commons, is the final scene's unqualified emphasis on parliament: parliament becomes, by force of the "lawful summons and authority" of the prince, the ultimate seat of government.[26]

Absolutism such as this of the first scene of the fifth act was not the political doctrine of all Englishmen in the mid-sixteenth century. It could scarcely have been Thomas Norton's doctrine. For Norton was a Calvinist; and, probably earlier in the year in which he composed his share of *Gorboduc*, he had, in bringing to a close his translation of Calvin's *Institutes*, written these sentences, which occur at the end of the remarkable and quietly revolutionary fourth book of the *Institutes*, entitled "Of outward means to salvation":

For though the correcting of unbrideled gouernement be the reuengement of the Lorde, let us not byandby thynke that it is committed to us, to whom there is geuen no other commaundement but to obey and suffer. I speake alway of private men. For if there be at this time any Magistrates for the behalfe of the people . . . I do not forbidde them according to their office to withstande the outragyng lycentiousnesse of kynges, that I affirme that if they winke at kynges wilfully ragyng ouer and treadyng down the poore communaltie, their dissembling is not without wicked breache of faithe, bicause they deceitfully betray the libertie of the people, wherof thei know themselues to be appointed protectors by the ordinance of God.[27]

In this fashion Calvin subtly defeats the theory of divine right of kings by giving similar divine right to magistrates. Thus Norton's position in regard to the succession could have been this: if Elizabeth's neglect of the matter could be construed as a raging over and treading down of the commons, then Norton, as a member of the House of Commons was justified in withstanding this "licentiousness" on her part. Practically, of course, such construction could scarcely be put on Elizabeth's inaction.[28] But in the final scene of the play the sense that the magistrate is obligated, even against the will of the sovereign, to protect the commonalty, is unmistakable.

4.

Since the political morality of *Gorboduc* must be but a reflection of the moralities of the men who wrote it, we are justified in grafting into our account some relevant biography.

In the year of the composition of the tragedy, 1561, Sackville had probably already written his *Induction* and *Buckingham*,[29] of which the former is certainly a distinguished precursor of *The Faerie Queene*, both in respect to its smooth and deftly archaic verses and its lofty allegorizing of virtues and vices. In 1561 Norton's translation of the *Institutes* came from the press, a book of a thousand blackletter pages, each trenchant and each dangerous to the older order of things; it was followed the next year by a second edition. In 1561 there also appears, in Sir Thomas Hoby's translation of Castiglione's *Courtier*, a commendatory sonnet by Sackville; a few lines from it will illustrate Sackville's predilection for the splendors of royalty and for the Italian manner in poetry:

> These royall kinges, that reare vp to the skye
> Their pallace tops, and deck them all with gold:
> With rare and curious workes they feede the eye:
> And shew what riches here great princes hold . . .[30]

The sonnet is as worthless in its way as Norton's minor poems; it is a piece of graceful artificiality, the point of the conceit being that Castiglione's work is richer and rarer than that of kings. There is nothing Italianate or graceful in Norton's metrical psalms, which also were printed for the first time in 1561; they are simply a serious, rough-and-ready contribution to a reform project begun in Edward VI's reign.

Sackville, in the year of *Gorboduc*, was twenty-five

years old. He was precocious: favored by birth—he was related to Elizabeth, and his father was a Privy-Counsellor under Edward and Mary as well as under Elizabeth—Thomas had been lavishly educated, had been a member of parliament, and had won a reputation in the newer school of poetry, that is, in the Italianate school promoted by Tottel. His father in all respects belonged to an earlier generation; frugal, conservative, and homely, Sir Richard Sackville was nicknamed in his county Sir Richard Fill-sack. Consequently Sir Richard was probably only seeking moral support for his own convictions when, in talking in 1563 with Roger Ascham about ways and means "to keepe yong men from licencious liuyng," he drew from Ascham a condemnation of "the fansie that many yong Ientlemen of England haue to trauell abroad, and namely to lead a long lyfe in Italie." [31] In spite of this disapproval and notwithstanding wife and children, who could not be taken along, Thomas Sackville went this year to Italy, where before he returned three years later he was imprisoned briefly, either at the order of his father for general extravagance or else for the particular extravagance of proclaiming too loudly his approval of the English church.

One other activity of Sackville has a bearing on *Gorboduc*. Shortly before 1570 the authors, according to John Day, prepared the manuscript of their tragedy for the authorized edition; thus, if Day is trustworthy, Sackville must have given attention again to the play at a time when he was occupied in another way with the problem of the succession. For in 1568 and again in 1571 he was in France attempting to arrange with Catherine de' Medici for the marriage of her third son, the Duke of Anjou, with Elizabeth. Of the embassy of 1571, which was intended as well to congratulate Charles IX for his marriage, Holinshed writes:

. . . as his ambassage was great, so was his charge no less, in furnishing himself and train accordingly, being both in number and furniture such in every point, as did appertain unto his character; and his receiving and entertainment in France, by the King and others, was agreeable thereto . . . He was banquetted by diverse, and that very sumptuously; which by him was not left unrequited to the uttermost, and rather with the better; for his liberality unto the French was very large, but his reward at the King's hands was only a chain, weighing a thousand French crowns . . .[32]

In his will Sackville remembers his part in arranging the secret treaty of marriage as what he calls "a matter of great trust and importance." [33]

The ambassador to whom the arrangements were entrusted could hardly have been unfavorable to the project. Yet the marriage would have united Elizabeth with a Roman Catholic family, albeit one that pretended at times to some moderation in its treatment of protestants; and we know how sharply Spenser opposes such a marriage in *Mother Hubbard's Tale*. Sackville, therefore, could have been in agreement with Norton that the succession was a problem of great moment, but it is altogether unlikely that his could have been the ardently protestant voice which, in the final scene of *Gorboduc*, pleads so openly for the appointment of Lady Katharine Grey as the successor of Elizabeth.

That voice could well have been Norton's, for Thomas Norton was as completely protestant as anyone in England. Norton had been secretary to Protector Somerset, he had married a daughter of Cranmer, and after Cranmer had been burned at the stake, the marriage of the widow united Norton's household with that of Edward Whitchurch, the influential puritan printer. When Norton was twenty he entered into a correspondence with Calvin which culminated in the translation of the *Institutes*. He published many Calvinistic tracts, and urged fervently on parliament the sanctioning of Cranmer's Calvinistic system of ecclesiastical reform. Later, as licenser of the press in London, he conducted examinations of accused authors so vigorously that the Catholics bestowed the title *archicarnifex* upon him; he is said to have boasted that he stretched a Jesuit on the rack until he made him a foot longer than God had arranged for him to be. He was so much a puritan that in 1574, in an exhortation to the Lord Mayor in connection with the plague, he shows himself strongly opposed to the public stage—to the "unnecessarie and scarslie honeste resorts to plaies, to shewes to thoccasion of thronges and presse, except to the servyce of God; and especiallie the assemblies to the unchaste, shamelesse and unnaturall tomblinge of the Italion Weomen . . .: to offend God and honestie is not to cease a plague." [34]

But he, too, had a connection other than that of *Gorboduc* with the movement to limit the succession. Just a year after Elizabeth had seen *Gorboduc* played, she was waited on by the whole House of Commons and presented with a petition for such limitation. This petition had been read in the commons two days earlier by Norton, who also, in all likelihood, was the author of it. It is in effect the last scene of *Gorboduc* thrown into oratorical form; its substance is this:

[Your majesty's late sickness has moved your subjects to frame a petition] for establishing some certain limitation of the imperial crown, for the preservation of your subjects from certain and utter destruction . . . They cannot, I say, but acknowledge your maj. hath most graciously considered the great dangers, the unspeakable miseries of civil wars, the perilous intermingling of foreign princes with seditious, ambitious and factious subjects at home, the waste of noble houses, the slaughter of peoples, subversion of towns; intermission of all things pertaining to the maintenance of the realm, unsurety of all men's possessions, lives and estates; daily interchange of attainders and treasons . . .

Your maj. hath weighed the examples of foreign nations, as what ensued the death of great Alexander, when for want of certain heirs by him begotten, or appointed, the variety of titles, the diversity of dispositions in them that had titles, the ambition of them that under colour of doubtfulness of title forsook all obedience of titles, destroyed his dominions, and wasted posterity with mutual wars and slaughters . . .

We have been admonished of the great malice of your foreign enemies, which even in your lifetime have sought to transfer the dignity and right of your crown to a stranger . . . we fear a faction of heretics in your realm, contentious and malicious Papists . . . lest they . . . lay in wait to advance some title, under which they may revive their unspeakable cruelty, to the destruction of goods, possessions and bodies, and thraldom of the souls and consciences of your faithful and Christian subjects . . . ; we see, on the other side, no such danger to your maj. by ambition of any apparent heir established by your benefit and advancement, for want of issue of your maj.'s royal body . . .

[There follow the modern examples of France and Scotland and a general appeal.] [35]

This petition like the conclusion of *Gorboduc* presents the extreme anti-Catholic position of Norton and the puritans. At other times parliament urged the conciliatory project, that of marriage, in which Sackville was soon to be active.

Biography predicates the view that Norton wrote the parts of *Gorboduc* which are preponderantly puritanical in politics. Biography likewise favors the general view that Norton wrote the scenes in which interest in practical politics is uppermost, while Sackville contributed those in which the interest is mainly esthetic and dramatic. Such a view is a general principle of this study; specifically this chapter intends to modify William Griffith's information that Norton wrote the first three acts and Sackville the last two, by proposing that the last scene of the play is by Norton and the first scene by Sackville.[36] But these proposals can be supported best by the more concrete evidence of diction and style.

5.

Criticism of the poetic language of *Gorboduc* has almost without exception come to a halt in the blind alley of "Senecan diction." H. Schmidt and his successors in this phase of study find neither discrepancies in diction between the parts of the play nor any variation in what appears to them to be a uniform exploitation of the Senecan vocabulary. But a greater burden of proof rests on these critics than they have thus far been willing to assume; for evidence that Seneca is the source of the diction of *Gorboduc* is valid only when more immediate sources have been examined and rejected. The language of the Bible, for instance, must have come more readily to the tongues of the authors, or most certainly to Norton's tongue, than that of either the Latin or the translated Seneca. So in this connection, probably for the first time since Warton allowed himself his outburst of impatience, we shall glance at the psalms which Norton versified shortly before he set to work on the tragedy.

The Senecan critics have picked from the play a series of passages in which references to blood and carnage resemble lines in Seneca. The following are examples:

> Thus fatall plagues pursue the giltie race,
> Whose murderous hand, imbrued with giltlesse blood,
> Askes vengeaunce still before the heauens face,
> With endlesse mischiefes on the cursed broode.
>
> (III, Ch., 13–6)

Oh cruele wight! should any cause preuaile
To make thee staine thy hands with brothers bloud?
(IV, 2, 135–6)

Is all the world
Drowned in bloud and soncke in crueltie?
(IV, 2, 169–70)[37]

While the phrasing of Seneca is often parallel to that of these lines,

Rudem cruore regio dextram inbuit. (*Tr.* 220)

Hominum cruenta caede pollutas manus . . . (*Oct.* 423)

. . . hinc terras cruor
Infecit omnes fusus, et rubuit mare. (*Hip.* 551–2)[38]

yet these "Senecan" images also appear, for example in Psalm 106:

To fiendes their sons and daughters they
did offer up and slay.
Yea with unkindly murdering knife,
the guiltlesse bloud they spilt:
Yea their owne sonnes and daughters bloud,
without all cause of guilt.
Whom they to Canaan Idols then,
offered with wicked hand:
And so with bloud of innocents
defiled was their land.
Thus were they stained with the works
of their owne filthy way . . .
Therefore against them lifted he
his strong reuenging hand:
Them to destroy in wildernesse,
ere they should see the land.
And to destroy their seede among

the nations with his rod . . .
And in his so enkindled wrath
the plague upon them broke . . .[39]

Here, collected into a few verses from a single psalm, is a richer "Senecan vocabulary" than that of Seneca himself; for in addition to the favorite Senecan words such as *blood* and *stain* and *hand*, the word *plague* appears both here in the psalm and in the lines from *Gorboduc* above; the phrase *guiltless blood* is common to both, and the expression *murdering knife* is paralleled in *Gorboduc* by *slaying knife* (V, 2, 151) and *revenging sword* (V, 2, 51). In this psalm, moreover, the theme of divine vengeance occurs just as it does in *Gorboduc:* vengeance is regarded as an act of punishment which extends into later generations.

One school of critics has gone so far as to formulate the principle that frequent appearances of the word *blood* and the personifications of *hand* and *heart* in early tragedies are tests of Seneca's influence.[40] Norton's psalms, however, and other of the Psalms, as well as other parts of the Bible and there is no telling how much more literature, use characteristically this same vocabulary and these same rhetorical devices. Consequently, since these tests, if they are to prove anything, must be supported by other evidence, we may turn to other aspects of the problem of Senecan influence on the ideas and language of this play.

"Nemesis," H. A. Watt declares, "and what Courthope calls the 'moving necessity of the family curse' are almost as apparent in *Gorboduc* as in Seneca."

Professor Watt continues: "The idea of a Nemesis, of an overhanging Fate which controls the destiny of mankind, is one of the commonest themes in Seneca . . ." [41] But Nemesis, thus adequately defined, does not come into *Gorboduc* at all. What does come in is the divine vengeance which we noticed in the psalm above. As a concrete case for analysis, an important and typically "Senecan" speech will serve. At the beginning of Act III, King Gorboduc, learning of the civil war undertaken by his sons, cries out:

> O cruel Fates! O mindful wrath of goddes!

He then runs through a catalog of instances of the wrath of the gods. The list is at once a manifestation of the medieval fondness for classical allusions and at the same time a parallel with the "notable examples" with which the petitions of parliament are swollen: for, it should not be forgotten, the victims at Troy, for instance, were King Gorboduc's legendary ancestors.[42] The fates and gods, moreover, are the simplest of poetic devices, and are probably no more exclusively Senecan than are the abundant classical allusions in the *Induction*.[43] And at the end of this speech the significance of the peculiar phrase "*mindful* wrath of gods" is unmistakable:

> Yet, O ye goddes, if euer wofull kyng
> Might moue ye, kings of kinges, wreke it [vegeance] on me
> And on my sonnes, not on this guiltlesse realme!
> (III, 1, 22–4)

In other words, the vengeance of the gods is conceived of here as divine retribution for specific faults; instead of retribution, the Senecan Nemesis is a curse, the origins of which lie in a deterministic universe and are unknown to those upon whom it is visited.

Support for this important distinction could be gathered in quantities from the early "tragical" literature. And, inasmuch as *The Mirror for Magistrates* is literally a series of illustrations of "how God plagued evil rulers," it is not quite reasonable to suppose that Sackville, a moving spirit in *The Mirror*, would have regarded *Gorboduc* from a basically different angle. It happens also that Lydgate has commented on heavenly vengeance in connection with a "tragedy" which has certain resemblances to *Gorboduc:*

> This tragedie be cleer inspeccioun
> Openli declareth in substaunce,
> How slauhtre of princis causith subuersioun
> Off rewmys, cites put out off ordynaunce,
> Off mortal werre long contynuaunce . . .
> The fyn declaryng off moodre & fals tresoun:
> The deede horrible crieth ay vengaunce
> To God aboue to caste his eien doun,
> To punshe this synne thoruh his myhti puis-
> saunce . . .[44]

In their version of Lydgate's philosophy, Sackville and Norton seem merely to substitute the names "fates" and "gods" for God. And these names, I believe, are broadly classical rather than narrowly Senecan; certainly the real morality of *Gorboduc* is the reverse of Senecan morality: witness the concluding speech—

> Yet must God in fine restore
> This noble crowne vnto the lawful heire;
> For right will alwayes liue and rise at length,
> But wrong can neuer take deepe roote, to last.[45]

It is said that Sackville and Norton imitated passages of sententious moralizing from Seneca. Several instances given by Watt are short rhetorical periods on the theme of royal lust for kingdoms: each contains the specific statement that the ambition of kings knows no law. Seneca begins, in the relevant passage, with a particular proposition: "Lex alia solio est, alia privato in toro," and then develops the idea of royal privilege in general terms.[46] Though the lines in *Gorboduc* are similar to those of this passage, a number of considerations make the "imitation" doubtful. In the first place Seneca makes a flat statement of a truism: he merely says that a king is a law unto himself. *Gorboduc* is saying, on the other hand, that ambition is lawless and exceedingly dangerous to the realm; and if a certain amount of rhetoric on this subject and in these terms is Senecan, then most Elizabethans and their forefathers before them spoke endlessly from the mouth of Seneca.

The passage which most resembles Seneca in phrasing, moreover, has been wrenched out of its context by the Senecan critics. Actually it is a scathing invective against monarchic ambition. It is satiric—a fact not mentioned by the critics; spoken by an evil counsellor who is but a scarcely disguised vice from the moral plays, it lays open the evils of ambition by seeming to praise ambition. Any broad sententiousness that it may have, could scarcely be less than the effect of the satiric purpose. And what should be very certain is that the bitter ring in the words of this passage carries down even to our ears in this day, when we too are not unmindful that in our age there is "in men the greedy mind to power, in worldly stage the stateliest parts to bear." The poetry of the passage is excellent, the question of debt to Seneca important; this is the passage:

> Know ye that lust of kingdomes hath no law:
> The goddes do beare and well allow in kinges
> The thinges [that] they abhorre in rascall routes . . .
> Murders and violent theftes in priuate men
> Are hainous crimes, and full of foule reproch;
> Yet none offence, but deckt with glorious name
> Of noble conquestes, in the handes of kinges.
>
> (II, 1, 143–5; 152–5)

It is worth the remark that the Elizabethan translator of the proposed source for this passage, John Studley (1566), so little understood the original, or was so little interested in it as a sententious truism, or was so enchanted with the Senecan context, that four out of his six lines have lost even the faintest grounds for a comparison with *Gorboduc*.[47]

To support this claim of Senecan sententiousness in *Gorboduc*, Professor Watt records only three more parallel passages. Of these one is again on the dangers of ambition; another is a two-line passage which appears to contain a purely accidental similarity; and the last is the lines on the "giddy commons" which were noticed earlier in this chapter. Watt compares the lines on the giddy commons at one place with Seneca, at another place with Virgil, and at a third place, just after he has granted that the play may echo the *Induction*, with lines in *Buckingham*.[48]

And indeed any passage which castigates popular fickleness may find numerous parallels in earlier literature. Seneca must not be ignored completely. This is especially true since Sackville himself has left a memorandum, scribbled at the end of the manuscript recently published by Marguerite Hearsey, which appears to read as follows:

> Remember Magister Burdeus [?] promise for the showing of Senecas chore [?] touching the captation of auram popularem.[49]

On the other hand when Sackville wrote the lines in *Buckingham* which seem most nearly to anticipate those in *Gorboduc*, it is quite clear that he had models other than the Senecan tragedies in mind. For Miss Hearsey has shown that Sackville's digression on the giddy people, the "commontie," was most likely suggested by Lydgate's treatment of Scipio and by examples in Valerius Maximus' *Dictorum et Factorum Memorabilium;* the identity of Sackville's illustrations —Camillus, Scipio, Miltiades, and Hannibal—with those in Lydgate and Valerius is at least very strong evidence of such connection; and Sackville, moreover, wrote the name *Valerius Maximus* on the margin of the manuscript at a later place in the poem.[50] In any event, to revile the masses was commonplace. The Senecan scholars have been at fault in tracing this theme back *exclusively* to Seneca.

Nor is there much to show that *Gorboduc* in form is welded exclusively, or even at all very securely, to the Senecan tragedies. The English play, it is true, has five acts, but several circumstances indicate that this mode of division may, in greater likelihood, have been derived from the classical comedies. For in the early sixteenth century the fusion of classical form with native medieval traditions is most evident in the school comedies, in *Ralph Roister Doister*, for instance; and these comedies moreover were composed directly to be acted on a stage. In comparison with comedy, English tragedy was a late development, and Seneca probably always remained primarily an author to be "read by candle light" rather than to be played. It is to be expected consequently that comedies had a greater influence on the processes of preparing a piece, like *Gorboduc*, for the stage than did tragedies. In this period, too, the names comedy and tragedy were of broad and imprecise significance, and the genres themselves were not distinct. Again, Seneca's tragedies, both in England and in Italy at this time, were not divided into scenes; but comedies in general were. Those divisions in the Senecan tragedies which we now call scenes are marked always by the entrance of a new character or characters; this is the structure neither of *Gorboduc* nor of the earlier English classical comedies. The method of announcing a new character in *Gorboduc*—

Loe, yonder comes in hast
Philander from my lord your yonger sonne.
(III, 1, 57)

—does not, as it does in Seneca, introduce a new scene. But it comes in the midst of the scene, as it does in the comedies:

But yond commeth Roister Doister nowe, in a traunce.
(III, 3, 5)

Finally, two *parasites* figure in the action of the tragedy; and, although they play the parts of vices in the moralities or moral plays, the name given them points exclusively to comedy.

Gorboduc is also structurally like a moral play in that good and evil counsellors, who are given tag-names, vie with each other for the favor of the central characters. The authors use long monologues where Seneca would have rendered the speeches in a dramatic form, often with the aid of a confidant; in this the authors are probably following the technique of the metrical tragedies as well as of the moralities. The monologues themselves, when they are political, reproduce the structure of a formal oration so exactly that even Sir Thomas Wilson's elaborate scheme of oratorical rhetoric applies to them.[51]

Gorboduc also, it is said, lacks a protagonist and consequently, unity of action; said in other and doubtless in better terms *Gorboduc* makes the commonwealth the protagonist. In this, a most important point in form, this tragedy is probably closer to the moral play *Respublica* (1553) than to any other play. For *Respublica* also aimed to show "how commonweals ruin and decay when wrong takes place of right"; and the author also makes his drama apply to the contemporary political situation. The characters are given abstract names and rôles: Respublica (really the Commonwealth of England) is a widow whom Vices, led by Avarice in the guise of Policy, delude; she is rescued from her difficulties by the Four Daughters of God, Misericordia, Veritas, Justitia, and Pax. *Respublica*, like *Gorboduc*, is divided into five acts with scenes.[52]

And so, to cast our immediate accounts, we may venture to propose that *Gorboduc* is a play made up of a diversity of elements. There may prove to be some patches of Senecan rhetoric in it: I should not care to propose that there definitely are none, but I am very certain that any such unmistakably Senecan elements would turn out to be less prominent than are identical elements in Sackville's *Induction* and *Buckingham;* and it is notable that Marguerite Hearsey, in her excellently grounded edition of these poems, makes illuminating comparisons with Virgil and Douglas' version of Virgil, with Boccaccio and Lydgate, with Valerius Maximus and other authors, but none at all with Seneca. It would seem that the Senecan critics, in order to substantiate their special case, have still to show that the diction and rhetoric and ideas of *Gorboduc* are not essentially traditional and that its form is not derived more importantly from the metrical tragedy, moral play, and comedy than from Seneca's tragedies.

6.

Painful examination of Senecan influence is necessary because *Gorboduc*, like a number of old plays, has been so thickly hedged round by criticism that it is difficult to see the characteristics and peculiarities of its ideas and of its poetry.

One trifling and indeed rather ludicrous point in its diction assumes a significance of certain proportions in connection with the problem of authorship. This is the use of the affirmative particle *yea*. To certain lines in some scenes of the play, *yea* lends a small explosion of emphasis. Now, *yea* also stands prominently in the lines of Norton's psalms and of his early poetry and also in his speeches. It is, of course, a Biblical expression; and as such it was doubtless shunned, consciously or unconsciously, by people who were not puritans, and Sackville was not a puritan. Actually it appears only once and then in a different sense in Sackville's extensive *Induction* and *Buckingham*.[53] Both Norton and Sackville, moreover, share in the habit of using a similar particle, *loe*. Consequently it seems certain that the use of *yea* is a mannerism, a habit, which was both peculiar and natural to Norton, and that the scenes in *Gorboduc* in which *yea* turns up are his.[54]

These scenes, it happens, are also marked by the frequent appearance of a special type of blank verse line, an end-stopped line made up of two symmetrical parts joined by a conjunction or preposition, each part consisting essentially of a substantive modified by an adjectival word. Professor Frank G. Hubbard remarked some years ago that the occurrence of this grammatically balanced line is a characteristic of the early regular tragedies; he found that it was most frequent in *Gorboduc* and that it appeared with decreasing prominence in the later tragedies.[55] An example of the line is the following:

> With furrowed face and with enfeebled lymmes.
> (I, 2, 105)

It is possible, I think, to go a few steps farther, to enlarge the specifications for the type, to tell something of its history, and something of its rhetorical effect.

In 1551 at the time of the revival of interest in *Piers Plowman*,[56] Norton published some verses which begin with these lines:

> Wee may wyte, if wee wyll, by holy writ
> The lore of the lorde, that ledeth to lyfe:
> Wee may see, if wee seche, and fynde in it
> The fall of falshed, the stenching of strife . . .[57]

This, of course, is alliterative "tumbling verse." Later on he composed another poem, which, though scarcely better as poetry, clearly indicates a development of the first style:

> Stay, gentle friend, that passest by,
> And learn the lore, that ledythe all:

From whence they come, with haste to gye,
To live, to die, to stand, to fall . . .[58]

Both of these passages show a strong tendency to alliteration, to internal balance, to end-stopping. Now these are precisely the characteristics of many passages in *Gorboduc*—of this one, for example:

Your *l*asting age shalbe their *l*onger stay;
For cares of kynges that *rule*—as you haue *ruled*—
For *publique* wealth and not for *priuate* ioye
Do wast mannes lyfe, and hasten crooked age
With *f*urrowed *f*ace and with en*f*eebled lymmes
To draw on *creepyng* death a *swifter* pace.
(I, 2, 100–5)

The homogeneity of the style can be summarized by putting three lines, each from the three examples of Norton's work, side by side:

The *l*ore of the *l*orde, that *l*edeth to *l*yfe.

And *l*earn the *l*ore, that *l*edyethe all.

But *l*onge may they *l*earne, ere they begyn to rule.
(*Gor.* I, 2, 232)

Consequently I think that the grammatically balanced line described by Professor Hubbard is to be extended to include alliteratively symmetrical lines, and that it originates in alliterative tumbling verse, passes through an intermediate stage in the four-stressed regular line, and becomes the characteristic end-stopped rhetorical line of the early tragedy. Alliteration in it, it might be noticed, is different from

Sackville's practice in that it always produces an end-stopped effect.

The practical value in identifying lines of this type is that they provide a definite key to Norton's part in *Gorboduc*. They indicate that Norton wrote the last scene of the play and all of the first three acts with the exception of the introductory scene.[59] This division is also supported by the occurrence of the mannerism *yea* and by the political considerations which we noticed earlier.

7.

Such a division gives Norton the hotly political and puritanical scenes, those scenes which are, besides, closest in structure to the moral plays and to the forms of political oratory, and in which esthetics is secondary to morality. The kind of rhetoric which we have assigned to Norton is not, however, to be dismissed lightly: the balanced, alliterative, end-stopped line is the line which we hear when Tamburlaine is threatening the world in his mightiest voice,

> And scourging kingdoms with his conquering sword.

In fact, it is doubtless true that the verse of the despised psalmist is the direct progenitor of the grand atheistic bombast which came in the next generation.

Nor is Norton's own contribution to *Gorboduc* despicable. Though his passion is rougher than Sackville's and by no means so finely drawn, it doubtless goes deeper. His voice has a greatness of its own when he pleads for his vision of social justice; and in his sense of England, the native land, he seems to anticipate Shakespeare:

> A ruthefull case, that those, whom duties bond,
> Whom grafted law by nature, truth, and faith
> Bound to preserue their countrey and their king,
> Borne to defend their common-wealth and prince,
> Euen they should geue consent thus to subuert
> Thee, Brittaine land, and from thy wombe should
>   spring,
> O native soile, those that will needs destroy
> And ruyne thee, and eke them-selues in fine!
> (V, 2, 15–22)

The tone of Sackville's contribution, on the other hand, is set by the opening lines of the play.

> The silent night, that bringes the quiet pawse
> From painfull trauailes of the wearie day,[60]
> Prolonges my carefull thoughtes, and makes me blame
> The slowe Aurore, that so for loue or shame
> Doth long delay to shewe her blushing face . . .

These lines have a movement, a purely lyrical movement, it will be noticed, like the beginning of the *Induction*, whence they go back to Gavin Douglas' prologues and thence into the pure stream of medieval, dream-vision, and allegorical poetry.[61] And Sackville's part in *Gorboduc* is notable for its insight into the possibilities of dramatic writing. It contains for instance the thoroughly articulate and soundly psychological soliloquy of the Duke of Albany, and also the vivid account of the death of Porrex, which Charles Lamb admired. And there are in it inconspicuous lines of subtle merit; these, for example, advise how the rebellion of the common people should be put down:

> Perswade by gentle speach, and offre grace
> With gift of pardon, saue vnto the chiefe,
> And that vpon condicion that forthwith
> They yelde the captaines of their enterprise . . .
> This shall, I thinke, scatter the greatest part
> That now are holden with desire of home,
> Weried in field with cold of winters nightes,
> And some, no doubt, striken with dread of law.
> (V, 1, 86–96)

Gorboduc, then, taken as a whole, seems to throw into focus a complicated and lively picture of its times. It is a picture lighted by the flares of two diverse renaissances in poetry—the one, following on the recovery of *Piers Plowman*, stiff and moralistic; the other, following on the printing of Tottel's *Miscellany*, elegant and Italianate. And over these flares hangs the glow of the greater, classical renaissance; but around and behind everything are the comfortable, familiar lights and shadows of the Middle Ages. A Vice stalks through the first dramatic tragedy and is hissed by the audience —the printer has taken care to indicate the hissing in his typography. And then there enters a *nuntius* to tell a tale which gleams with blood and armor.

The puritan pleads for the welfare of the commons, while the courtier jibes at the rascal routs, but both come together momentarily in *Gorboduc* to urge preparations against a dubious political future. Probably only the deepest apprehension of the future could have enabled two men so fundamentally different to collaborate successfully; this, and their mutual zest for sheer creation in literature.

CHAPTER II

THE FORMATION OF THE HEROIC MEDIUM

GORBODUC, when all is said, must remain a simple play, aiming at simple purposes. The purely literary and rather sensational effects on the one hand and the ingenuous preachments on the other hand make it a not very difficult puzzle to solve. These tendencies towards showy effects and towards stiff didacticism persist, as we shall see, in the tragic literature of the next decades; and they are indeed the leading principles in that literature. But when they gradually disappeared, as they had to disappear, under the onslaught of much more complicated and valuable purposes, then it is no longer easy to correlate a dramatist's biography with his dramatic production; nor is it easy, in a time when the writing of drama became a career open to many closely associated authors, to distinguish one man's style from that of another man.

Since mounting complexity is thus to be expected in the later drama, some division of the subject, some simplification, is now in order. Consequently we proceed to an examination of the general problem of tragic style.

THE HEROIC MEDIUM

PART I

I.

Whenever a period has produced a fine and characteristic literature, it has used a fine and characteristic medium of expression. Aristotle is painstaking in describing the connections between the substance of tragedy, comedy, and the epic, and the poetic forms which they employ. We, in our day, are usually no less diligent. We say that the heroic couplet—the regular, antithetic closed couplet—is the embodiment of wit; and, if we are orthodox, we say that before Pope was born the heroic couplet was taking shape in the hands of Waller. We look at Corneille, and behind Corneille, in the same fashion. Such inquiry is not limited to the forms of classical poetry; it is perhaps most complete in connection with the work of the English romantic poets.

But in connection with the Elizabethan drama it has only been begun. There are, it is true, studies which deal more or less narrowly with the prosody of blank verse; [1] what is needed, however, is an account of the more-than-mechanical qualities of early unrhymed poetry—its relations to still earlier poetry, its rhetorical peculiarities, its affinity with certain subjects and with certain attitudes towards life; an account, in fine, of the complex qualities comparable with those which we recognize in the heroic couplet. This is the need which the present chapter will attempt to fulfill.[2]

It is intended to have a twofold relation to the other

chapters. On the theoretic side, in trying to isolate one of the formal elements of Elizabethan tragedy, I suppose that the principles underlying the formation of the medium of expression will apply to the general formation of tragedy: a history of heroic blank verse should be essentially a first sketch of the rise of English tragedy; for the tragic hero will be roughly what he is able to express in words. On the practical side I hope to contribute a clearer description of early poetic style and of its remarkable uniformity, to bring some small support to Sir Edmund Chambers' very important theory of a uniform "school of the 'eighties,"[3] and consequently to indicate a few of the hazards, already alluded to, of pronouncing a doubtful play, on the basis of style alone, this man's work or that man's work.

Poetical rhetoric does not lend itself easily to an obviously systematic analysis. I have thought it best to adopt a plan of this sort: to present first, as a point of reference for later discussion, a characterization of immediately pre-Shakespearean blank verse; to turn then to a chronological survey of the rise of the medium, and to inject into this survey some rather free comparisons of early and late examples; and finally, to give a more substantial account of the later practices.

2.

Professor Tucker Brooke, writing on "Marlowe's Versification and Style,"[4] has contributed a valuable and culminant essay to the numerous studies of Marlovian rhetoric. With some shifting of emphasis, Professor Brooke's paper will remain, I think, an important description of blank verse in a crucial stage of development. Its brief account of the pre-Marlovian stages, however, seems to me to be unsatisfactory.

The general feeling, in which Professor Brooke shares, is that before *Tamburlaine* blank verse was not native to the genius of the English language, that it was employed only when Englishmen were affecting to write like Romans, and that in Marlowe's hands it became instantly, as Hallam said,[5] the finest instrument that a tragic poet has ever employed.

Without denying Marlowe's genius for the medium, we may resist this tide of general feelings and sweeping claims. It is difficult to say how and when any verse form becomes native to the English language. I believe, and I think the following pages will show, that Marlowe did not change blank verse so much as he exploited to the limit a newly developed taste for it: the "mighty line" was born early; if it was hidden, as it often was, in a context of brittle, non-flowing lines,—that was what native English taste in the mid-sixteenth century demanded of verse in general. There are probably as good heroic couplets in Shakespeare as in Waller;[6] they are not conspicuous, are not used extensively, because taste had formed no predominant bent towards the intellectualizing and ironic effects of the closed couplet. When we talk about such elusive matters as the native genius of English, the only relevant question is whether the verse of *Gorboduc* was less effective than the best contemporaneous examples of tumbling verse or poulter's meter. I think it was not; this statement will come as no surprise to the readers of the first chapter of this study. I also think it possessed a few virtues of its own as well as the resources and defects of contemporaneous forms.

Later on we shall glance at the detail of the connections between English blank verse and Latin quantitative verse. But, as a matter of fact, all that should need to be said can be said in two sentences: Those poets, led by Gabriel Harvey, who consciously attempted to simulate the effects of the Romans did not regard blank verse, any more than rhymed verse, as a means to their ends. And the translators of Seneca, in their deliberate efforts "to keepe that Grace and majestye of stile, that Seneca doth,"[7] employed, in a project running from 1559 to 1581, every common meter except blank verse. The absence of rhyme is by no means a mark of the imitation of classical poetry; and conversely, blank verse was regarded no more than any other form as an equivalent to classical Latin verse.

Nor is it reasonable to suppose that blank verse in Marlowe's hands became instantly the finest instrument that the tragic poet has ever employed. Such things do not happen instantly. So extreme a view ignores the changes which Marlowe himself imposed, in his more mature years, upon the medium, not to mention the changes which Shakespeare imposed upon it. So sweeping a view tosses *The Spanish Tragedy* completely aside; and Thomas Kyd's contribution to early dramatic blank verse, though it may not be earlier than Marlowe's, is certainly an independent contribution and one that proved to be scarcely of less value to the maturing Shakespeare.

The history of the formation of blank verse is inevitably complicated. A medium which can give utterance to feelings of all shades and can sustain them, which can pursue complicated thought in all its delicate ramifications—such a medium must have roots which go deep and wide. It is the same with verse form as with dramatic form: there may be an occasional creaking and superficial imitation of Ovid or Seneca, but all that is essential to a line of poetry or to a drama will go so much deeper that the importance of the imitation is negligible. Blank verse, I am convinced, has its roots in medieval poetry. The evidence for this conviction will appear in a moment; meanwhile, I stress it on the grounds that it is probably the only reasonable view to take.

3.

But Christopher Marlowe brought unrhymed poetry suddenly to a state of crystallization. This is axiomatic. To do so, he limited blank verse practically to a single effect: poetic oratory. And in singling out this one effect from the many which had formerly accompanied it, he was compelled to subject drama itself to amazing limitations: he forced *Tamburlaine* into the narrow structure of a vehicle for declamation, and, to motivate so much declamation, he relied only on the spectacular device of giving limitless heroic grandeur to pride, the first of the deadly sins. *Tamburlaine*, in simplest terms, is pride-oratory.

Marlowe's achievement overwhelmed his contemporaries quite as much as it overwhelms students of the Elizabethan drama. Allusions to Tamburlaine's conquest of the stage are extraordinarily frequent between 1587 and 1592; though they are familiar, we shall glance at a few of them, for they serve admirably to characterize blank verse at a significant time and also to indicate the importance which dramatists placed upon the medium of expression.

The medium of expression, the blank verse of *Tamburlaine*, is what Marlowe himself emphasizes above all else.

> From iygging vaines of riming mother wits,
> And such conceits as clownage keepes in pay,
> Weele lead you to the stately tent of War,
> Where you shall heare the Scythian Tamburlaine
> Threatning the world with high astounding terms
> And scourging kingdoms with his conquering sword . . .[8]

We shall hear Tamburlaine threatening the world; we shall *hear* him scourging kingdoms. Elizabethan audiences heard him, and were content for awhile only to hear more. Dramatist Robert Greene, finding himself forced to earn his livelihood by writing a prose romance, protests against those who "had it in derision for me that I could not make my verses jet out upon the stage," and who "set an end of scollarisme in an English blanck verse." [9] This was in 1588.

The next year Greene's friend Thomas Nashe appealed to their university friends, Spenser, Peele, Watson, and others, to assist Greene in reforming this new and extravagant taste for rhetorical drama. After praising the "scoller-like shepheard" Greene, Nashe proceeds to lay his contempt on the writers of plays, who, he says, "intrude themselves to our eares as the alcumists of eloquence, who, mounted on the stage of arrogance, think to out-brave better pens with the swelling bumbast of a bragging blanke verse." He goes on to sneer at their "kill-cow conceits and the spacious volubilities of a drumming decasyllabon." [10] On the same occasion, the appearance of Greene's *Menaphon*, another of Greene's friends, in condemning the fashionable drama, sees fit to criticize it from the point of view of its verse:

> Come forth, you witts that vaunt the pompe of speeche
> And strive to thunder from a Stageman's throat;
> View Menaphon, a note beyond your reach,
> Whose sight will make your drumming descant doate . . .[11]

But Greene and Nashe and Lodge, in spite of early antagonism and humiliating failures, soon achieved their own successes in drama. They even came later to regard themselves along with Marlowe as the special masters of declamatory verse. So it happened that, in 1592, Greene could turn his fire against Shakespeare, the newcomer, the "upstart crow," who, Greene says wrathfully, "with his *Tyger's heart wrapt in a Player's hide* supposes he is as well able to bumbast out a blank verse" as the best of them.[12]

These contemporary remarks indicate that for a short period a definite style of verse was the greater part of drama. And it was—but with limits which can readily be defined. The generalization applies, of course, only to the popular stage; the style of Lyly, which was doubtless the predominant style in comedy, was fundamentally that preferred by the court. But in the favorite popular forms, tragedy and chronicle-history, rhetoric must have been especially important because other things were not important: plots were anybody's property, and plays rewritten for rhetorical ends were as much in demand as new plays; [13] the lack of complicated stage equipment must have caused the dramatists to be but little concerned with stage effects; and since the actors themselves attended to stage business and even improvised extensively, the dramatist's occupation was essentially a literary occupation. It was, it seems, Shakespeare's ability to bombast out a blank verse that got him his fellowship in a cry of players.

Blank verse, in this period, is consistently described as *bombastic*. This is essentially good description, except that actual bombast (cotton padding), since it was an accepted aid to tailoring, probably was not so derogatory a term as it is now. Gascoigne uses it as a figurative equivalent to flesh: "It hath no bumbast now, but skin and bones . . ." [14] Perhaps the overtones in the phrase "to bombast out a blank verse line" were something like this: "to tailor out a line." The intention, however, to suggest an inflated, if not padded line, comes out in the expressions *bragging*, *swelling*, *jetting*, *drumming*.

The structure of the blank verse line, which is really Marlowe's "mighty line," is also indicated rather strikingly, I think, in the dramatists' own references to their verse. The mighty line is, I believe, in its narrowest form a balanced line in which the first part plays against the last part either verbally or alliteratively and often in both ways; it is structurally the type of line which we noticed in the account of *Gorboduc*. Its features are conspicuous in the first lines of the prologue to *Tamburlaine:*

> From *iygging* vaines of *riming* mother wits.
> And *s*uch con*c*eits as *c*lownage *k*eepes in pay.
> And *scourging k*ingdoms with his *conquering* sword.

It appears again in the verse which Greene flings back at Shakespeare,

> his *Tyger's h*eart wrapt in a *Player's h*ide;

and the verbal balance is worked out perfectly in Shakespeare's original line:

> O *tiger's h*eart wrapt in a *woman's h*ide.

The dramatists seem even to be imitating this balanced line in their prose references to blank verse. They drop into alliteration and play noun and adjective against noun and adjective to the extent that, if it were not for the extra syllable, Nashe's

> the *swelling b*umbast of a *bragging b*lanke verse

would be, itself, a fine example of the mighty line.

Blank verse, then, in the year 1592—the year which marks the effectual end of the careers of Marlowe, Greene, and Kyd, and the beginning of the career of Shakespeare—blank verse is characterized by its deliberate cultivation of swelling rhetoric. It uses a strict decasyllabic line; [15] Marlowe's fairly frequent use of a final light eleventh syllable is practically limited to his practice of winding up a line with a resounding proper name. The stresses alternate regularly in the iambic fashion, with reversals in stress usually excluded from the body of the syntactically tight line. End-stopping is the rule; it is indeed the most notable principle of heroic verse at this time and perhaps the chief source of its strength. For effective run-on structure is a refinement and a subtilizing which was totally unsuited to the drama of Marlowe and most of his contemporaries.

These are fundamental specifications. There will be numerous irregularities, of course; but they are probably due merely to the oversights and compromises which accompany hasty writing.

4.

The mighty line of Marlowe is signalized, I think, by rhetorical balance. But I do not mean at all that every line in Marlowe, or that even a large proportion of lines, will conform to the type which I have described. In *Tamburlaine I* Professor Hubbard counts forty-four lines that have strict grammatical balance; [16] if we count those in which balance also results from alliteration or plays on words, the number will not be much more than doubled, will not be more than five per cent. But the number of these lines is not so important as their position: in position they stand like keystones and cornerstones in Marlowe's rhetoric. They may come as a climax to one of Tamburlaine's lofty periods:

> That perfect blisse and sole felicitie,
> That sweet fruition of an earthly crowne.
>
> (879–80)

Or more often they comprise the introductory steps, the exclamatory entrance to a lofty passage; this is the way in which Tamburlaine begins his speech at Zenocrate's deathbed:

> Proud furie and intollorable fit,
> That dares torment the body of my Loue,
> And scourge the Scourge of the immortall God . . .
>
> (3046–9)

The formula of the balanced line is, for Marlowe, a point of departure and a point of return. It seems consequently to be the norm in his rhetoric.

This brings up a question of method. It appears to me that in order to give an effective account of blank verse rhetoric, we are obliged continually to extract a series of norms from our specimens: we must find foundational lines and passages, foundational modes of articulating the passions. These will not necessarily represent an author at his best; indeed an author like Shakespeare may be most interesting when he departs from the norm. But we are interested in the formation of Elizabethan blank verse, rather than in the special excellences of a Shakespeare.

The problem is serious enough to justify an illustration.

In Shakespeare's *Richard III*, the scene in which Clarence is murdered is constructed in this fashion: Clarence, imprisoned in the tower, has had a marvelous dream which he recounts in great detail. The dream prognosticates his death; he prays that God, in punishing him, may spare his innocent family. Then he falls asleep, and the murderers enter. In semi-humorous terms they also speak of divine punishment. Awakening, Clarence pleads for his life on the grounds that vengeance belongs to God alone. He dies, though one of the murderers has relented.

Now this scene is a series of manipulations of the theme of divine vengeance. Clarence's prayer is the foundational passage in it, the norm for the rhetoric. For the dream leads up to the prayer, and after the prayer follow rhetorical variations on it, including the prose variations of the murderers. The lines that compose the prayer are these:

O God! if my deep prayers cannot appease thee,
But thou wilt be aveng'd on my misdeeds,

Yet execute thy wrath on me alone:
O! spare my guiltless wife and my poor children.
(I, 4, 68 ff.)

The lines preceding the prayer are richer poetry, but until they have been given a firm direction by the prayer, they must appear to be but a fine example of the tendency in the sixteenth century to exploit a common and beautiful and probably Virgilian theme; they have an evasive quality, as if the nervousness of Clarence is recapitulated in the form assumed by the lines themselves:

> I pass'd, methought, the melancholy flood,
> With that grim ferryman which poets write of,
> Unto the kingdom of perpetual night.
>
> . . . a legion of foul fiends
> Environ'd me, and howled in mine ears
> Such hideous cries, that, with the very noise
> I trembling wak'd, and, for a season after
> Could not believe but that I was in hell
> Such terrible impression made my dream.
> (I, 4, 45–7; 58–64)

And then, in the speeches of the murderers which come soon after the prayer, we find an excellent illustration of Shakespeare's ability to vary a theme and to fit it to vastly different personages. When the clownish murderer takes up the theme of divine punishment, Shakespeare shifts from the serious, formal blank verse of Clarence clear over into prose:

Sec. Murd. The urging of that word 'judgment' hath bred a kind of remorse in me.

First Murd. What! art thou afraid?
Sec. Murd. Not to kill him, having a warrant for it; but to be damn'd for killing him, from the which no warrant can defend me.

(I, 4, 108–14)

Clarence's prayer, obviously, is not in itself a purple patch; but it is a perfectly good example of early Elizabethan blank verse, of the norm in phrasing and in feeling. The old king Gorboduc speaks of divine vengeance in quite the same voice:

> Yet, O ye goddes, if euer wofull kyng
> Might moue ye, king of kinges, wreke it on me
> And on my sonnes, not on this giltlesse realme!
>
> (III, 1, 22)

And generally similar passages, in idea or in phrasing, are to be found in sixteenth-century literature wherever one starts turning pages.[17] Indeed, Tamburlaine's notorious challenge in which he "dares God out of his heaven" is, as it were, only the obverse of the conventional.[18]

Study of this sort of foundational and conventional rhetoric should provide us with a means, as limited as it may be, for generalizing about the unrhymed heroic medium.

5.

The preceding pages may serve as an elementary sketch of blank verse as it was when Shakespeare first began to use it. There must follow now some account of its formative stages; later on the sketch of it in its approach to maturity can be taken up again.

The value of a chronological study is increased enormously, however, if there is evidence of a definite continuity in the subject. Before *Tamburlaine*, blank verse, so far as we know, had made only a dozen appearances. How safe is it to assume that the later poets profited by the examples of the earlier poets? Does each new endeavor in blank verse become an influence on succeeding endeavors? I am convinced that the work of the poets of the sixteenth century shows an extraordinary continuity. This belief, I think, is generally accepted. There is also, it happens, concrete evidence to support it which is pertinent to the subject at hand. One bit of evidence is the use of the rare, and of course in itself unimportant, adjective *hugie* in special contexts. The strange word and its context appear in the poems of most of the authors with whom we are concerned. This could not happen by accident; it must be an indication of definite influences. Moreover, to glance at the appearances of the word is practically to epitomize the history of poetics and poetic relationships in the century.

Probably the first problem in early sixteenth century poetics is the question of the arrangement of stresses in the decasyllabic line. Wyatt seems to have had his ear, especially in his early work, attuned to a cadence which was radically different from the iambic movement;[19] Tottel had an ear only for the iambic movement, and, by his vigorous editing of the manuscripts which he published, he appears to have forced our present principles of metrics upon his contemporaries. Surrey counted syllables; but though he was often negligent or at least not rigorous, he does move towards a line which has a smooth flow of alternate stresses. His efforts in this direction are apparent in the lines in his translation of the *Aeneid* which have to do with the wooden horse of Troy. At first he writes:

> A huge horse made, hye raised like a hill.[20]

This awkward clutter of syllables—"a huge horse made"—results from his taking the phrase over bodily from Gavin Douglas' translation of the *Aeneid* into Scottish dialect:

> Ane huige hors, like ane greit hill, in hy.[21]

When Surrey encounters the phrase again he has more or less difficulty with it:

> Whereto was wrought the masse of this huge hors. (188)
>
> (Douglas: Onto quhat fyne this huge hors was heir.) (p. 76, 14)
>
> Yonder huge horse that stands amid our walls. (420)
>
> (Douglas: Within the wallis, yone mekle standand hors.) (p. 88, 8)

Then suddenly Surrey overcomes all his difficulties by adopting the rare form *hugie:*

> Clambe vp againe vnto the hugie horse.
> (512)
>
> (Douglas: Clam wp agane in the greit hors maw.)
> (92, 11)

And thus a Gordian knot in metrics was cut.

Other poets followed Surrey's example. Jasper Heywood, when he had occasion to mention the horse of Troy in his introduction to his translation of Seneca's *Troas* (1559), fashions this line:

> A hugie horse where many a warlike Knight
> Enclosed was . . .[22]

Here implications abound. Heywood was an unusual translator of Seneca in that, besides sharing in the universal interest in the medieval aspects of Seneca's morality, he also aspired most seriously to reproduce Seneca's "Grace and majestye of stile." [23] From all of Seneca's plays he selected the one that had to do with Troy; he was versatile in metrics and apparently familiar with Surrey's blank verse.[24] Yet he renders Seneca in nearly every form—fourteeners, rhyme royal, decasyllabic quatrains—but not in blank verse. Two years later *Gorboduc*, a play based on English history and occupied with a problem in immediate national politics, is written in blank verse. The inference is that unrhymed poetry had no associations in the minds of the poets with Latin quantitative verse.

Thomas Sackville, in his medieval and Virgilian marvelous journey, *The Induction*, sees the fall of Troy painted in the shield of the personification War; he exclaims:

The hugie horse within thy walls is brought.[25]

Farther along in the same poem he writes:

The wide waste places, and the hugie playne.
(St. 73)

And this line reappears with but slight changes in *Gorboduc:*

Let them beholde the wide and hugie fieldes.
(V, 2, 61)

The context for the adjective *hugie* has now broadened out. But that it remains an artificial literary word, a convenient poetic dissyllable, is indicated perhaps by its appearance in an alliterative, euphuistic, and ineffectual line, in its final occurrence in *Gorboduc:*

To see the hugie heapes of these vnhappes.
(V, 2, 109)

This is the phrase which Turberville retains in his translation of Ovid's *Heroides:*

And be enricht with hugie heapes of massy
gold so brave.[26]

Finally the word makes some notable appearances in the later drama. Marlowe, in writing

Your threefold armie and my hugie hoste,
(*Tam.*, 1192)

has retained the traditional alliterative context; and Sackville, moreover, had used precisely the same phrase in the *Induction:*

The hugie hostes, Darius and his power.
(St. 58)

The phrase reappears in *The Misfortunes of Arthur:*

> With hugie hoast withstoode him at the shoare.
> (II, 1, 58)

And Kyd, in a Virgilian description of hell which was doubtless influenced by Sackville's *Induction,* seems to paraphrase Sackville's line,

> The wide waste places, and the hugie playne,

with this line:

> Within a hugie dale of lasting night.
> (*S.T.*, III, 11, 21)

And a little later *Selimus* has, "Like hugie mountains do your waters rear" (1765); and *Locrine,* "Hercules that tamed the hugy monsters" (260).

The intention in writing at this length about an inconsequential little word was primarily to indicate how closely interrelated are the works of sixteenth-century poets. The theory of a "school of the 'eighties" seems to be sound enough indeed, but the school probably runs over the boundaries of the decade. Several things in addition are suggested too. One is that the moment Surrey got hold of his decasyllabic line it became in his hands and then in the hands of Sackville as good a line as the very good lines of Marlowe and Kyd, and in no way different from theirs. This observation excludes the matter of the total effects of passages, but it is none the less, from a rhetorical point of view, an important truth. Another implication is that the Virgilian tradition, especially in regard to the fighting in

Troy and Aeneas' descent into hell, is an influence of enormous vitality. And this, too, is an observation which should bear fruit later on.

PART II

1.

It is generally accepted now that Surrey found suggestion for an English blank verse in an unrhymed Italian version of the *Aeneid*, perhaps in that of Cardinal Ippolito de' Medici or his secretary, perhaps in that of Nicolo Liburnio. It is also accepted that the date of the experiment would lie between the years 1539 and 1547.[27]

To belabor the question where blank verse came from is unprofitable. The urge to write a rhymeless verse was a general Renaissance phenomenon, behind which lay, no doubt, the example of the ancients. It was an urge towards a refinement in poetics, not a revision of poetic principles. Thus Surrey's blank verse cannot be considered an imitation of classical measures; for the revision in poetics, to which Surrey like Wyatt was devoted, was the syllable-counting principle, and nothing could be more contrary to classical prosody. Surrey simply wrote his decasyllabics without rhyme. The influence of the Italians could have made crucial the question of rhyming or not rhyming; but the question itself is inconsiderable.

What is considerable is the diction, the phrasing, the organization of the verses. And in these regards, just as Surrey's poetry as a whole is as native as Chaucer's, his blank verse is cut from the best of traditional patterns. For at bottom it is Gavin Douglas' version of the *Aeneid* transformed into unrhymed heroics. Now Surrey was a capable scholar and a fine poet: he departs from Douglas when he sees fit, though with notable infrequency at first; and he does, as we shall see, make his own essential contribution.

But discussion of Surrey's verse ought to be grounded on some lines. Those that follow, as editors have noted, represent Surrey in a fairly dependent passage:

> Here Hecuba, with her yong daughters all,
> About the altar swarmed were in vaine,
> Like doues that flock together in the storme;
> The statues of the gods embracing fast.
> But when she saw Priam had taken there
> His armure, like as though he had ben yong,
> "What furious thought, my wretched spouse," quod
>   she,
> "Did moue thee now such wepons for to weld?"
> (II, 666–73)

Douglas had written:

> Hecuba thidder, with hir childer, for beild
> Ran all in vane, and about the altair swarmis,
> Brasand the godlik ymage in thair armis,
> As for the storme dowis flockis togidder ilkane.
> Bot quhen scho saw how Priamus hes tane
> His armour, so as thoch he had bene ying:
> Quhat fulich thocht, my wrechit spous and king,
> Movis ye now sic wapnis for to weild?
> (p. 99, 6–13)

And Virgil:

> Hic Hecuba et natae nequiquam altaria circum,
> praecipites atra ceu tempestate columbae,
> condensae et divom amplexae simulacra sedebant.
> Ipsum autem sumptis Priamum iuvenalibus armis
> ut vidit, 'Quae mens tam dira, miserrime coniunx,
> impulit his congi telis? Aut quo ruis?' inquit.
>
> (II, 515)

Perhaps the first remark should be that both the Englishman and the Scotsman do a creditable job of translating the Roman. Both retain something of the compactness of the Latin. Douglas' *swarmis* and *flockis* are happy condensings of implications; these Surrey has wisely retained. On the other hand there is loss in the omission of *atra*. The uneconomical locution *like as though he had been* is more troublesome in Surrey's English than in Douglas' dialect.

The second point must be that each of Surrey's lines is a version of a line in Douglas: the mere intention of translating the Scottish dialect into English iambic decasyllabics could scarcely have produced a closer version. It is also true, I believe, that if Surrey had used rhyme, he would have been forced to depart farther from his model, and the problem of writing his *Aeneid* would have been a different problem. This may have urged him in the direction of rhymeless verse.

In any event it was fortunate for Surrey that Douglas wrote a good strong line. For it must be apparent in the specimen above that the key-words, the impelling diction, as well as the syntactical structures are fundamentally Douglas'. Even Surrey's one run-on line comes from Douglas. Consequently I think there is no especial value in analyzing matters like *enjambement* and the *caesura* in Surrey's blank verse: these things will be the same (as indeed the findings of the prosodists have shown them to be) in all comparable verse of the period.

But there is also evidence here that Surrey has attained a mastery of the iambic decasyllabic period. He makes, for instance, an excellent line,

> Like doues that flock together in the storm,

out of one of Douglas' especially difficult tumbling-rhythmic structures.

Since this study is after all a sketch of sixteenth-century verse rhetoric, a comparison of Surrey's work with that of the much more popular Phaer is not out of place. The parallel passage is this:

> There Hecuba and her doughte[r]s all
> (pore soules) at the altars side
> In heapes together affrayd the*m* drew,
> like doues wha*n* doth betide
> Some storme the*m* headlo*n*g driue,
> & clippi*n*g fast their gods thei hold.
> But whan she Priam thus beclad
> in armes of youth so bold
> Espied: what minde alas (q*uo*th she)
> o wofull husband you
> In harneis dight: and whither away
> with wepons run ye now? [28]

Phaer is the translator of Virgil who received the laudations of his century; even George Peele calls him "the fairest Phaer that ever ventured on great Virgil's works."[29] It is perhaps only right for us to cry doggerel, as everyone does, and have done with this fourteener version. Yet there was a time when these lines were sincerely admired: I think it is possible to see that they are fuller, are more leisurely, more affecting, more mournful than those of Douglas or Surrey, and are not without their appeal. They are not bare and bold, they are not declamatory, not heroic. But the sixteenth century liked them, and that is one reason why blank verse came only slowly into prominence.

Translations of Virgil are especially important to us in that a preponderantly rhetorical drama like the early English tragedy makes extensive use of epic fragments and epic technique. An illustration will conclude our remarks on Surrey's verse and begin the transition to dramatic verse.

The splendid and influential passage which tells of the fall of Priam is turned by Surrey into these lines:

> Of Priamus this was the fatal fine,
> The wofull end that was alotted him,
> When he had seen his palace all on flame,
> With ruine of his Troyan turrets eke.
> That royal prince of Asie, which of late
> Reignd ouer so many peoples and realmes,
> Like a great stock now lieth on the shore;
> His hed and shoulders parted ben in twaine,
> A body now without renome and fame.
>
> (721–29)

The relationship to Douglas can now be made perfectly clear; for Surrey is following Douglas here with what appears to be, in Book II, neither more nor less than his usual closeness. Douglas wrote:

> Of Priamus thus was the finale fait;
> Fortune heir endit his glorius estait
> Seand Ilion all birning in firis broun,
> And Troyis wallis fall and tumblit doun;
> That riall prince, wmquhill, our Asia,
> Apone sa fell pepill and realmis alsua
> Ringit in weltht, now by the coist lyis deid
> Bot as ane stok, and of hakkit his heid;
> A corps, but life, renowne, or wthir fame,
> Vnknawin of ony wycht quhat was his name.
>
> (101, 5–14)

Most of the essentials, I think, go back to Douglas, but this difference becomes apparent now: Surrey is studiously condensing the Douglas text. It is not that Douglas is prolix; the little elaboration on Virgil which occurs in the last lines is the really guiltless mark of the medieval moralist, and quite in keeping with the marginal note that Priam's fall is an "Exempyll of the infellicitye and inconstant fortune of the kingdomis of this world." But Surrey in his last lines gives utterance to the pure classic spirit, and in clear heroic lines. This is Surrey's greatness.

Technically he is as we have described him. The impelling diction is Douglas' and so is the general movement. Even details like alliteration and the very successful run-on structure going into "Reignd ouer . . ." come from Douglas. So it is back in Gavin Douglas and the felicitous Scottish traditions that English blank verse takes its source.

One aspect of the epic technique comes out in the recital of Priam's fall: the device of combining in one sentence the glories of the past and the woes of the present, the royal prince and the dead stock. Now in one of the most famous pages of *Gorboduc*, Marcella's report of Porrex's death, the foundational rhetoric is built upon precisely this same combination of glory and wretchedness. These are Marcella's central lines:

> Alas, he liueth not! It is to true
> That, with these eyes, of him, a perelesse prince,
> Sonne to a king, and in the flower of youth,
> Euen with a twinke a senselesse stocke I saw.
> (IV, 2, 199–202)

The diction here, it will be noted, contains interesting reproductions of Surrey's diction in the passage above. The contrast of Porrex's brilliant youth and his miserable end, which is developed throughout Marcella's long recital, is remarkably parallel with that which forms the structure of Surrey's lines written about his imprisonment in Windsor ("So crewell prison . . ."). Surrey, after comparing his childish years to those of "Priams sonnes of Troye," composed several lines like those given to Marcella—e.g.:

> . . . with sleves tyed on the helme.
> (Surrey, p. 84)

> . . . thy mistresse sleue tied on thy helme.
> (*Gor.*, IV, 2, 251)

The language of Marcella's narrative is sensational, and has been called Senecan; but Seneca's way of handling similar recitals, as for instance the report of Hippolytus' death, is to pile horror on horror with no contrasting elements; for, since his aim is to show that life is utterly ruinous and despicable, misfortune cannot come as a contrast to past glory—there is no glory. On the other hand there were enough sensations in Virgil's account of the fighting in Troy—which Douglas calls a "deidlie Tragedy" [30]—to satisfy even the avidity of the sixteenth century for horror; and there were these other things besides.

2.

Four years before *Gorboduc* was written, Nicholas Grimald also had occasion to tell of the fall of a heroic character, Marcus Tullius Cicero, "of royall robe, and sacred Senate prince." Cicero, like Porrex, becomes a "senslesse stock."

> Popilius flyeth, therwhyle: and, leauyng there
> The senslesse stock, a gryzely sight doth bear
> Vnto Antonius boord, with mischief fed.[31]

Grimald used blank verse for his epic fragment.

Grimald contributed this piece, "Marcus Tullius Ciceroes Death" (88 lines), and another blank verse piece, "The Death of Zoroas" (115 lines), to Tottel's *Miscellany;* he translated the former from Theodore Beza's *De Morte Ciceronis*, and the latter from Gautier de Chatillon's *Alexandreis*, which, in turn, seems to have been influenced by Lucan. And Lucan, as is well known, is one of the chief patrons of epical expression in the sixteenth century.

The blank verse of "The Death of Zoroas" is jagged and ejaculatory. It does contain a few resounding balanced lines like those which, under the influence of *Piers Plowman,* were soon to make their way into *Gorboduc;* this one, for instance, occupies a telling position as the concluding line of the poem:

> From derk obliuion of deuouryng death.

But the exclamatory descriptive passages are remarkable and puzzling. For, on the one hand, Grimald's jaggedness results apparently from a direct transposition of Gautier's medieval Latin into English. And on the other hand, a swift, rough narrative seems to have been traditional in accounts of battles: Grimald's technique resembles Chaucer's in *The Knight's Tale,* and Chaucer's extraordinary manner here is thought to go back to the alliterative romances.[32]

Whatever may have gone before Grimald's lurid and explosive lines, a great deal of important poetry comes after them. I am about to suggest that the epical description of the battle, with which Kyd opens the action of *The Spanish Tragedy,* is modeled on them; I am persuaded in part to do this because Tottel's *Miscellany* was probably the most important of literary works in its times, certainly the most popular of the books containing blank verse: it went through seven or possibly eight editions in the thirty or so years preceding *The Spanish Tragedy.* Grimald wrote in part as follows:

> Now clattering arms, now ragyng broyls of warr
> Gan passe the noyes of dredfull trompets clang:

> Shrowded with shafts, the heuen: with clowd of darts,
> Couered, the ayre . . .
>
> Now corpses hide the purpurde soyl with blood.
>
> Shaking her bloody hands, Bellone, among
> The Perses, soweth all kindes of cruel death.
> With throte ycutt, hee roores: hee lyeth along,
> His entrails with a launce through girded quite:
> Him smites the club, him wounds farstryking bowe . . .[33]

Kyd:

> Both cheerly sounding trumpets, drums, and fifes,
> Both raising dreadfull clamors to the skie . . .
>
> Now while *Bellona* rageth heere and there,
> Thicke stormes of bullets ran like winters haile,
> And shiuered Launces darke the troubled aire . . .
>
> Heere falles a body scindred from his head,
> There legs and armes lye bleeding on the grasse,
> Mingled with weapons and vnboweld steedes,
> That scattering ouer spread the purple plaine.[34]
>
> (I, 2, 28–9; 52–4; 59–62)

I shall not pause to point out the reproduction here of arrangement, words and images, except to note that Kyd's obscure phrase "purple plaine" is clarified by Grimald's additional "with blood." Very probably Kyd's abrupt "here—there" construction is a holdover from Grimald's (and Chaucer's) inordinately abrupt "he—he" constructions. On the other hand Kyd has obviously succeeded in straightening out Grimald's contorted lines.

Marlowe was devoted to variations on these themes.

For him they provided substance for Tamburlaine's most extravagant threats:

> Our quiuering Lances shaking in the aire,
> And bullets like Ioues dreadfull Thunderbolts,
> Enrolde in flames and fiery smoldering mistes,
> Shall threat the Gods . . .
>
> (616–9)

> So shall our swords, our lances and our shot
> Fill all the aire with fiery meteors.
>
> (1495–6)

In another similar context (1246–56) Marlowe makes a direct reference to Pharsalia; this is only a slightly less direct reference to Lucan, and, since we are dealing here with the epical element in dramatic poetry, it has its importance to us. At two other places (1474 ff.; 3192 ff.) Marlowe combines imagery of the troubled air with elaborate astrological material; this has a possible significance too, for in Grimald's poem, immediately after the descriptive lines quoted above, twenty-four consecutive lines are devoted to astrology, to the erring stars and the fates. Marlowe, in his usual fashion, motivates his rhetoric with a simple reversal of precedents: Tamburlaine holds the fates bound fast in iron chains.

The conspicuous epic strain in the relatively early drama has, I think, the immediate ancestry which I indicate above—a Douglas-Surrey-Grimald ancestry. This is at variance with accepted theory. According to Dr. Boas, for instance, Kyd's description of the battle is derived from Garnier.[35] Now it is true that

Garnier wrote a very similar narrative in Act V of *Cornelie;*[36] the similarity, however, is probably due to Garnier's own cultivation of Latin epical traditions. And a more serious difficulty follows upon the theory of Garnier's influence: the association of Kyd and Garnier brings up the connection of Garnier with Seneca (which in itself is by no means so close as is generally thought[37]), and by virtue of a hasty syllogism *The Spanish Tragedy* becomes a Senecan drama and this particular scene a Senecan scene with the report of a messenger. Over against this artificial construction, these are the important facts, I think: (1) since Kyd does not preserve the unities, a messenger's report is not an organic necessity to his play; (2) epical battle passages are common to both Marlowe and Kyd; (3) as will be shown later, Kyd utilized a number of poetic traditions, all of which are strictly literary and not dramatic; (4) Kyd, in adopting the unrhymed medium, directs it towards the same effects and the same ends as do the most available of his predecessors; (5) the influence of the classics on Kyd, as indeed on all of his contemporaries, is complex: ultimate sources for a passage like that in question are more likely to be found in Lucan or Virgil than in Seneca.

3.

After Surrey's accomplishment and Grimald's laborious contribution, it is of some interest to find that blank verse was next exercised—so far as is known—by one of the authors of *Gorboduc* shortly before

Gorboduc itself was written.[38] For Thomas Norton, in translating Calvin's *Institutes of the Christian Religion,* adopted blank verse as a means of rendering into English the portions of Virgil which had been quoted by Calvin. Norton's translation of Calvin's work was first published on May 6, 1561; *Gorboduc* was presented for the first time at Christmas in 1561. It is fairly certain that Norton had completed his translation before *Gorboduc* was written: this is commonly accepted as a fact on the basis of the difference between the above dates; and since *Gorboduc* was composed to provide "furniture of part of the grand Christmasses in the Inner Temple,"[39] it seems that Sackville and Norton must have written the play fairly late in 1561.

In the fifth chapter of Book I of the *Institutes* Calvin quotes from Virgil's *Aeneid*, Book VI, lines 724–731. Norton translates this passage as follows:

> Fyrst heauen, and earth, and flovvyng fieldes of seas,
> The shinyng globe of Moone, and Titans starres,
> Sprite fedes vvithin, and throughout all the lymmes
> Infused mynde the vvhole huge masse dooth moue,
> And vvith the large bigge body mixe it selfe.
> Thense come the kyndes of men and eke of beastes,
> And lyues of fliyng foules, and monsters straunge,
> That vvater beares vvithin the marble sea.
> A fyry lyuelynesse and heauenly race there is
> VVithin those seedes. &c.

And Calvin quotes immediately after this from the *Georgics*, Book IV, lines 219–227, which are translated by Norton:

Some say that bees haue part of mynde diuine,
And heauenly draughtes. For eke they say, that God
Gothe through the coastes of lande, and crekes of sea,
And through depe skye. And hense the flockes and
heardes:
And men, and all the kyndes of sauage beastes,
Eche at their byrthe receyue theyr suttle lyues.
And therto are they rendred all at laste,
And all resolued are retournde agayne.
Ne place there is for deathe: but lyuely they
Flye into nombre of the Starres aboue,
And take their place vvithin the lofty skye.

These lines in themselves contain few points of especial interest. Like Grimald's, they are stiff decasyllabics. They employ, however, a fairly successful variation on the end-stopping principle in that the *enjambements* are marked sometimes by a heavy stress on the first syllable of the second line; this device serves to preserve the integrity of the individual lines, to prevent the blurring which results from careless *enjambement.* The two extra syllables in the next to the last verse from the *Aeneid* are probably a printer's error, which also went uncorrected in the revised edition of 1562.

Since it has always been assumed—and most reasonably, I think—that rhymeless verse was suggested to the authors of *Gorboduc* by the example of Surrey, these twenty-one lines may be regarded as the positive link between Surrey's blank verse and the blank verse of *Gorboduc:* these lines seem indeed to be a perfect proof of continuity.

4.

Certain prominent rhetorical features of *Gorboduc* seem to have sprung directly from Sackville's *Induction,* and that is to say, from the vast and highly ornamented "vision" literature of the Middle Ages. These features may be gathered under two convenient heads —the symbolic landscape and the elaborately visualized personification. They are often intermingled.

What I mean by the symbolic landscape and the elaborately visualized personification, as well as the mode of treatment to which they are subjected, can be illustrated by these splendid lines of Sir David Lyndsay, which appear in the Prologue to the *Dreme:* [40]

> I met dame Flora, in dule weid dissagysit,
> Quhilk into May wes dulce, and delectabyll;
> With stalwart stormis, hir sweitnes wes surprisit;
> Hir hevynlie hewis war turnit into sabyll,
> Quhilkis umquhile war to luffaris amiabyll.
> Fled frome the froste, the tender flouris I saw,
> Under dame Naturis mantyll, lurking law.

Here Lyndsay is establishing a setting for a poem which is remarkably parallel with Sackville's *Induction.* Both poets find themselves in a sad winter scene; both poets, conducted by a personification-guide, go on a marvelous journey into hell; and both utilize the marvelous journey as a means for dramatizing the vices of their native lands.

Sackville begins by describing the sorrowful winter landscape:

The wrathfull winter proching on apace,
With blustering blastes had all ybarde the treene,
And olde *Saturnus* with his frosty face
With chilling cold had pearst the tender greene:
The mantels rent, wherein enwrapped beene
The gladsom groues that now lay ouerthrowne,
The tapets torne, and euery blome downe blowne.

Sackville here and in the next few stanzas seems to be borrowing from one of Gavin Douglas' characteristically medieval prologues to the books of the *Aeneid;* he transposes Douglas' dialect into his own smooth, slightly archaic English in much the way that Surrey had done before him. The third line, for instance, seems to be condensed from these lines of Douglas: [41]

Rany Orioune wyth his stormy face . . .
Frawart Saturne, chill of complexioune . . .

Sackville's debt is known to all students of his work. But I think it has never been noticed that his rhyme royal stanzas have an intricate movement which is also, in all likelihood, derived from the Scottish poets. A comparison of the passages from Sackville and Lyndsay above shows that the end-stopped lines of both poets are modified in that they are parts of larger syntactic structures, which are marked by a harmonious interweaving of phrases and relative clauses.

The verse of *Gorboduc* in some scenes—in those scenes especially which seem to be Sackville's—reproduces not infrequently the harmonies of the rhyme royal stanza. The best illustration is doubtless to be found in the opening lines of the play.

> The silent night, that bringes the quiet pawse
> From paineful trauailes of the wearie day,
> Prolonges my carefull thoughtes, and makes me
> blame
> The slowe Aurore, that so for loue or shame
> Doth long delay to shewe her blushing face;
> And now the day renewes my griefull plaint.

Thus *Gorboduc* opens with a continuation of the verbal, grammatical, and metrical practices of the *Induction* and the great Scottish works; and to the same end: the first lines of *Gorboduc,* in their reference to natural phenomena, are setting the tone, the *mood* of what is to follow.[42]

But such writing does not come to very much in the first regular tragedy. It lay fallow for another quarter century, and then, for Thomas Kyd, it yielded magnificently. For Kyd, realizing fully what was natural all along to the medieval "vision" literature, the expression, namely, of emotion in terms of a symbolic landscape or symbolic journey—Kyd took these materials and made of them the metaphors in which his characters express their feelings. To describe how he did this will be an objective of the final pages of this chapter.

Some of the most striking pages in Sackville's *Induction* are devoted to highly visualized portraits of abstract vices—Remorse, Dread, Revenge, Misery, Care. . . . Pure personifications, of course, are of ancient lineage—one thinks of Fame in Book IV of the *Aeneid* and Philosophy in *The Consolation of Philosophy*—and Sackville's personifications are suggested by Virgil's account of the descent into hell. But the English poet has developed his figures along strictly medieval lines; Remorse, Dread, Revenge, and the rest are closely related to the Seven Deadly Sins as the sins are treated by Dunbar and the author of *Piers Plowman.* Now, in *Gorboduc,* in the dumb show and the chorus attached to Act IV, there is a description of the furies—

> The dreadfull Furies, daughters of the night,
> With serpentes girt, carrying the whip of ire,
> With heare of stinging snakes, and shining bright
> With flames and bloud, and with a brand of fire.
>
> (IV, Ch. 11–14)

—which seems to reproduce the portrait of Debate, painted on the shield of War, in the *Induction:*

> Deadly *Debate,* all full of snaky heare,
> That with a bloudy fillet was ybound . . .
>
> (St. 58)

This suggests that the "Senecan" furies in *Gorboduc* are of complex origin; and if we consider other descriptive passages in the *Induction,* such as this of the "fat weeds" that rot on Lethe wharf—

> A deadly gulfe: where nought but rubbish grows,
> With fowle blacke swelth in thickned lumpes that lies,
> Which vp in the ayre such stinking vapors throws
> That ouer there, may flie no fowle but dyes . . .
>
> (St. 31)

—or if we examine the sensationalism and the blood in the many passages like these in the *Complaint*—

His head dismembred from his mangled corps,
Her selfe she cast into a vessel fraught
With clottered bloud of them that felt her force.
(St. 14)

The launsed spear hee wrythes out of the wound,
From which the purple bloud spins on his face . . .
(St. 21)

—we must conclude, I think, that the vast body of sensational Elizabethan rhetoric is not of specifically Senecan origin.[43]

The chief rhetorical accomplishment of *Gorboduc*, however, is the declamatory, balanced alliterative line to which we have already given much attention. Since the description of the way in which Norton developed this line out of alliterative tumbling verse, has already been presented,[44] it will suffice here simply to compare a few typical lines from *Gorboduc* with later examples of the line. The line which we used in our earlier comments on *Gorboduc*,

But *l*onge may they *l*earne, ere they begyn to rule,
(I, 2, 232)

may be compared with *Tamburlaine*, 734:

And *gladly* yeeld them to my *gracious* rule;

And *Gorboduc*, I, 2, 104,

With *furrowed face* and with *enfeebled* lymmes,

with *Tamburlaine*, 660:

The *fainting* army of that *foolish* king.

Kyd follows the same rhetorical principle:

> Where *wounded* Hector liues in *lasting* paine.
> (*S.T.*, Ind. 48)

The rhetorical principle is applied here, moreover, to a line which Kyd seems to have imitated from Sackville's *Induction*,

> Not wurthy Hector wurthyest of them all,
> (St. 65)

and Sackville's line itself is an illustration of another principle of alliteration, that is, one which does not result in a balanced structure.

In fact, after *Gorboduc*, lines of this kind began appearing everywhere. It is significant, for instance, that an able editor of Samuel Daniel's poetry, Arthur Colby Sprague, in two out of three examples of Daniel at his best, selects lines which follow the same rhetorical pattern:

> O cleer-eyde Rector of the holie Hill.
> Thys sorrowing farewell of a dying kisse.[45]

Professor Sprague points out the perfection of these lines, and compares the last with Marlowe and the Ovidians. This suggests some generalizations: The later sixteenth century sought for and attained a mastery of the single line. In it polish and balance are exceptionally noticeable; consequently, though it appears to have sprung from *Piers Plowman*, it is also suitable to the sophisticated purposes of the Ovidians, and has an intrinsic character not unlike that of the eighteenth century couplet. But it comes to another peak in the broad declamatory heroics of Marlowe.

5.

Balanced rhetorical lines are especially conspicuous in *Jocasta*. And this is no great wonder, for *Jocasta* in all essential respects seems to be a reflection of *Gorboduc*. Actually, of course, George Gascoigne and Francis Kinwelmarshe translated their tragedy from the Italian of Lodovico Dolce, who in turn had followed a Latin version of Euripides' *Phoenissae*. Thus only very indirectly was it a Senecan play; for the sixteenth century it was a Greek play notable for its morality.[46] But the translators worked with a certain freedom, and herein they showed not so much originality as dependence on *Gorboduc* their heightening of effects seems to be inspired by that play.

Jocasta was written during the year following the first publication of *Gorboduc*. It resembles the earlier play in the following respects: it uses the same theme (a reason for its selection for translation?)—civil war between two brothers; it was also presented to an Inns of Court audience; it moralizes further than the Italian version on the same commonplace sources of worry—monarchic ambition, the rashness of youth, the pains of civil war; it adopts blank verse and along with blank verse the dumb show for the second time in the regular drama; and it employs consistently the highly stylized rhetoric of the earlier play, e.g.:

Joc.:

With stretching string, or else with bloudie knyfe.
(II, 1, 71)

Gorb.:

By strangling cord and slaughter of the sword.

(V, 2, 9)

Joc.:

Alas, alas, how wrekeful wrath of Gods.

(II, 1, 131)

Gorb.:

That,—if the mindfull wrath of wrekeful gods.

(II, 2, 75)

Joc.:

For crooked age and hory siluer heares
Still craueth helpe of lustie youthful yeares . . .
But rest a whyle thy weake and weary limmes.

(III, 1, 23–4; 28)

Gorb.:

For cares of kynges that rule—as you haue ruled—
Do wast mannes lyfe, and hasten crooked age
With furrowed face and with enfeebled lymmes.

(I, 2, 101; 103–4)

Joc.:

Euen so amidde the huge heape of my woes.

(II, 1, 116)

Heape one mishap upon anothers head.

(V, 3, 37)

Gorb.:

To see the hugie heapes of these vnhappes.

(V, 2, 109)

These lines are meant to illustrate the unvarying resemblance of *Jocasta* to *Gorboduc* in regard to alliteration, euphuism, vocabulary, and sensational phraseology. The examples above are by no means exhaustive;

I have merely noticed the parallels for lines from *Gorboduc* which, for one reason or another, we have referred to earlier in this study.

The rhetoric of *Jocasta* is that of *Gorboduc* extended and elaborated, forced not too impressively to a higher pitch. *Jocasta*, as indeed *Gorboduc* too, exploits the clichés of the sixteenth century—clichés which are common to the metrical psalms, the authorized homilies, the Senecan plays, Surrey's Virgil, the miscellanies, and also Dolce's play; typical examples of them are expressions like "just revenge," "guiltless blood," "dreadful death," "slaughtering sword," etc.[47] Expressions of this kind are in themselves bombastic; they doubtless provided a stimulus to the formation of the bombastic heroics of the later dramatists. As an illustration of this we might consider the famous lines of Tamburlaine in which he commands the burning of the town in which Zenocrate died. In part they are the following:

> So, burne the turrets of this cursed towne,
> Flame to the highest region of the aire . . .
> Threatning a death and famine to this land,
> Flieng Dragons, lightning, fearfull thunderclaps,
> Sindge these fair plaines . . .
>
> (3191 ff.)

Behind these lines there seems most certainly to lie a complicated tradition of rhetoric. It is probably founded in part on the Biblical plagues; at least in *Gorboduc* this version of the curse sounds very much like the Bible:

Thus shall the wasted soile yelde forth no fruite,
But dearth and famine shall possesse the land!
The townes shall be consumed and burnt with fire,
The peopled cities shall waxe desolate.
(V, 2, 225–8)

But it is also classical, as in *Jocasta:*

And angry *Mars* shall ouercome it all
With famine, flame, rape, murther, dole and death:
These lustie towres shall haue a headlong fall,
These houses burnde, and all the rest be razde.
(III, 1, 137–40)

6.

We come now to a series of examples of early blank verse which I believe did not have any very direct influence on the rhetoric of tragedy, but which are relevant here because they help, by antithesis, to define the heroic style.

Turberville's selection of blank verse in 1567 as a medium in which to render six of Ovid's *Heroides* was probably inspired by the fact that he was dedicating his work to Lord Thomas Howard, the younger brother of the Earl of Surrey. Turberville is a most interesting and admirable poet in his way: he is a precisionist, a meticulous filer of phrases, sophisticated and practically precious in his devotion to Anglo-Saxon monosyllables. A moment's reflection on the part played by full, round multisyllable words in Marlowe's line, or for that matter in Shakespeare's or Milton's, will show why Turberville is at his best in his favorite meters—fourteeners and poulter's meter—rather than in blank verse. His lines tend to break up in small fragments:

> At length, of Sire, his servants, and the day
> Dreading: these words to break thy sleepe, I spake.[48]
>
> (p. 176)

His studious intellectuality is perhaps best exhibited in the singular poem, "The Translator to the Captious Sort of Sycophantes," which he appended to his *Heroycall Epistles*, of which this is a significant stanza:

> Devises of the language divers are
> Well couched words and feately forged phrase,
> Eche string in tune, no ragged rime doth jarre,
> With figures fraught their bookes in every place:
> So that it is a worke of prayse to cause
> A romaine born to speake with English jawes.
>
> (p. 342)

Dramatic blank verse, of course, demanded something larger, and at first something looser and plainer, than Turberville's featly forged phrases. His poetry, though it frequently glitters like barbaric jewelry, does not become the stageman.

George Gascoigne, in his blank-verse poem, *The Steel Glas* (1576), is a precisionist of a different stripe. He shares his contemporaries' propensities to alliteration, balanced lines, quibbles, euphuism; but he makes two individual departures from their practices: he is a stern advocate of parallel structure and a *caesura* after the fourth syllable. Neither of these principles, if it is held to as rigidly as Gascoigne holds to it, is congenial to dramatic heroics.

Yet Gascoigne has notable convictions as to the special properties of the unrhymed medium. In his prefatory poem, which I think has never been discussed in this connection, he says he aspires, with all due modesty, to lasting fame as a poet; but the tower of fame, on which he has his eye, is much too tall "for ladders made of ryme." Therefore he will try to batter it down:

> Such battering tyre, this pamphlet here bewraies,
> In rymelesse verse, which thundreth mighty threates,
> And where it findes that vice the wall decayes,
> Even there (amaine) with sharpe rebukes it beates.
> The worke (thinke I) deserves an honest name,
> If not: I fayle to win this forte of fame.
>
> (II, 140)

The metaphor is mixed. But it is clear that Gascoigne has realized, possibly because of his experience with *Jocasta*, that blank verse is a suitable medium in which *to thunder mighty threats;* and this characterization, coming as it does at least ten years before the prologue to *Tamburlaine*, makes the whole picture-puzzle of early blank verse history fall into shape: *Tamburlaine* is not the bolt out of the blue that it has been thought to be.

There still remains the question why Gascoigne wrote *The Steel Glas* in its peculiar kind of blank verse. The prefatory poem suggests Horace perhaps, and Professor Brooke has written that Gascoigne "appears to be aiming at the ostentatiously pedestrian elegance of Horace's *Sermones*." [49] On the other hand the metrical features of the poem and conspicuous allusions in it indicate that it is much influenced by *Piers Plowman;* it is also very strikingly the same kind of poetry, both in point of satiric-moral purpose and parallel structures, as that which Gavin Douglas wrote in several prologues in the *Aeneid,* especially in the one before Book VIII. But this prologue was strongly influenced by alliterative poetry, and it itself is paralleled by much more medieval poetry. Certainly to find Horace in the bulk of *The Steel Glas* is to run far afield.

The question of relations between the English sixteenth century poets and the Latin poets demands another word. Professor Brooke finds that each important early example of unrhymed verse is an imitation of a Latin measure: Gascoigne is imitating Horace; the authors of *Gorboduc* and of *Jocasta* "are apparently seeking to give the impression of the Senecan senarius";[50] most of the other examples speak for themselves since they are translations; in fact "the un-English character" of Surrey's versification "is noted on the title-page of the second edition of Surrey's work (book iv), which calls it a 'straunge meter.' "[51] The last statement must be an error; the 'straunge meter' is from the first edition of the translation (1554), at which time the meter was indeed strange.[52] The other points come essentially to this: *Gorboduc* is motivated essentially by a passionate interest in English political morality; the most careful and literary of the translators, Turberville, favors the older meters rather than blank verse.

These men were all experienced and gifted poets.

This means that to write with or without rhyme would involve them in no creative difficulties: they would choose one form or another at will; all depended on the effects they wished to produce, and for the studied, ink-horn poetry of the sixteenth century, rhyme was most suitable. Heroics had to wait for a stage on which to be declaimed. Allusions to the classics do not mean direct imitation; comparisons with the Latins, as Francis Meres amply proves, do not mean imitation either. Every poet hopes that his work will compare with that of the Ancients. But no poet who aspires to such comparison will want, or will be able, to divorce himself from the poetic disciplines which have been handed down to him.

7.

For the sake of completeness I enter here a list, which I copy largely from Professor Brooke's article, of the remaining minor examples of blank verse that can be said positively to antedate *Tamburlaine:*

Spenser (?): Fifteen 'sonnets' in Van der Noodt's Theatre, 1569.

Barnabe Riche: A poem (170 lines) in *Don Simonides*, 1584.

Peele: *The Arraignment of Paris* (parts only), 1584.

"Lines to Th. Watson" (11 lines), prefatory to Watson's *Hekatompathia*, 1582.

"The Device of the Pageant before Wolstan Dixi" (the opening speech only: 53 lines), 1585.

Of these only one item is of significance, and it, I am sure, is of the highest significance. It is the blank verse in Peele's *Arraignment of Paris*, especially Paris' "Oration to the Council of the Gods." The oration begins:

Sacred and just, thou great and dreadful Jove,
And you thrice-reverend powers, whom love nor hate
May wrest awry; if this, to me a man,
This fortune fatal be, that I must plead
For safe excusal of my guiltless thought,
The honour more makes my mishap the less,
That I a man must plead before the gods,
Gracious forbearers of the world's amiss,
For her, whose beauty how it hath enticed,
This heavenly senate may with me aver.
But sith nor that nor this may do me boot,
And for myself myself must speaker be,
A mortal man amidst this heavenly presence;
Let me not shape a long defence to them
That ben beholders of my guiltless thoughts.
(IV, 1, 66 ff.)

Here the oratorical manner of *Gorboduc* has swung back fully into the drama. In these fifteen lines one-third are marked by the balanced structure which has been practically the theme of this chapter, and along with the balanced structures are traces of the familiar clichés and quibbles. The decasyllabics are of full heroic length, ringing, polished, yet suitable to the stageman's throat. Paris' words express a decorum proper to a mortal man defending himself before the gods; but it is a verbal decorum: the tone is Tamburlaine's.

The tone and the manner are more than that; they are the tone and manner of the tragic hero defending himself before a hostile or somehow remote audience.

> Then for the deed,—that I may not deny,
> Wherein consists the full of mine offence,—
> I did upon command; if then I erred,
> I did no more than to a man belonged.

Peele has brought the rhetoric of the "one-may play" to its full stature. For blank-verse rhetoric, in being essentially oratorical-declamatory, predicates a peculiar relationship between the speaker and the listeners; the listeners must be placated and won over, or scourged with threats. The speaker stands alone; the hero tries to enforce or to clarify and to reconcile his relationship to a contrary world. This is one good reason why there was a one-man drama, and a good reason for at least one aspect of Othello's rôle:

> Most potent, grave, and reverend signiors,
> My very noble and approv'd good masters,
> That I have ta'en away this old man's daughter,
> It is most true . . .

There is very little to add now to the foregoing remarks on Marlowe, the Marlowe at least of *Tamburlaine*. One point of interest, however, is that the direction taken by some of the most extravagant rant points back to the old popular drama. Oaths like this of Baiazeth,

> By *Mahomet*, my Kinsmans sepulcher,
> And by the holy *Alcaron* I sweare,
> He shall be made a chast and lustlesse Eunuke . . .
> (1173–5)

probably have behind them as a stimulus the ravings of Herod, although the lines themselves are clearly formed according to the heroic pattern. Similarly it is doubtless true that the bombastic Oriental drama of Greene and Peele drew some of its verve from the religious pageants.

The method used in these pages has neglected, of course, a consideration of the possibilities of general, extended effect; and Marlowe, it is perfectly evident, by turning upside-down the sin of pride and the overawing influence of fate, achieved a motivation for sustained effects of startling power and beauty. This is not to insinuate anything about the morality of *Tamburlaine:* we could call it an amoral rhetorical drama, but there is also some certainty in the proposition that *Tamburlaine* is a moral drama in that it opposes licentiousness, effeminacy, "Italian pleasures"—that is to say, the vices embraced by Tamburlaine's opponents and by Gaveston.

Marlowe also made positive strides in the development of eloquent and articulate metaphors. But a discussion of this aspect of blank-verse rhetoric will come out best in connection with the work of Thomas Kyd.

PART III

A good deal of the rhetoric of *The Spanish Tragedy*, it would appear, is derived from the metrical tragedy embellished with the marvelous journey and the graphically described, complaining ghost. And this rhetoric is not always ignoble: I hope that the following paragraphs will show that Kyd, despite possible intentions to write only sensationally, tapped one of the purest streams of English poetry, and at times, at crucial times, turned its current to what modern readers are obliged to call the most worthy of purposes.

For Kyd took materials like those which appear in Sackville's *Induction*, a marvelous journey, and *Buckingham*, a tragical complaint of a ghost, and made of them the language of his characters' mental anguish. This is to say, he reduced these traditional materials to figures of speech which could convey the personal emotions of a Hieronimo or an Isabella; and to credit him with this, is practically, in view of chronology, to credit him with an important contribution to the development of the great Elizabethan language of metaphors.[53]

This process of forming figurative language is particularly clear in the passages in which Hieronimo mistakes the Old Man for the ghost of Horatio. At first Hieronimo accepts the Old Man as a ghost as real as any who visited the bedchambers of the writers of metrical tragedies:

> And art thou come, *Horatio*, from the deapth,
> To aske for iustice in this vpper earth . . .?
>
> Sweet boy, how art thou chang'd in deaths black shade . . .
> *Horatio*, thou are older than thy father . . .
>
> (III, 13, 132 ff.)

But when the Old Man refuses to admit that he is either the ghost of Horatio or a Fury sent to guide

Hieronimo into the infernal regions, Hieronimo makes this most interesting speech:

> Thou art the liuely image of my griefe;
> Within thy face my sorrowes I may see.
> Thy eies are gum'd with teares, thy cheekes are wan,
> Thy forehead troubled, and thy muttring lips
> Murmure sad words abruptly broken off
> By force of windie sighes thy spirit breathes . . .
> (III, 13, 161 ff.)

Hieronimo still seems to be taking the Old Man for an apparition; an apparition in fact which bears a close resemblance to Sackville's ghost of Buckingham, who with "vapored eyes upcast" thrice "began his doleful tale, and thrice the sighs did swollow up his voice." But for Hieronimo this is no longer a good solid ghost; it is a *lively image of grief*.

Thus it was Kyd, it would appear, who made the transition from the "filthy whining ghost" of the metrical tragedies to the Shakespearean ghost, to whom such words as these are addressed:

> Thou canst not say I did it: never shake
> Thy gory locks at me.

For what is this but a lively image of Macbeth's guilt? Or when Brutus, troubled in thought and bent over his book late in the night (familiar prelude to a ghost!), discovers the dead Caesar standing before him, and says,

> I think it is the weakness of mine eyes
> That shapes this monstrous apparition,

what the audience really sees is not the Ghost of Caesar but an outward manifestation of Brutus' state of mind.

Hieronimo also expresses his great sorrow by imagining that he will go on a marvelous journey down into hell where he will plead for justice and revenge. Sometimes he thinks a Fury or a Personification will act as guide for him, and sometimes, seeming at a loss to know what to do for a guide, he calls upon such a person as the Old Man to play Orpheus. Needless to say this is an adaptation of the regular business of the medieval poems. The following passage is one of many:

> *Hieronimo*, tis time for thee to trudge:
> Downe by the dale that flowes with purple gore,
> Standeth a firie Tower; there sits a iudge
> Vpon a seat of steele and molten brasse,
> And twixt his teeth he holdes a fire-brand,
> That leades vnto the lake where hell doth stand.
> Away, *Hieronimo;* to him be gone:
> Heele doe thee iustice for *Horatios* death.
>
> (III, 12, 6 ff.)

This should be entirely recognizable despite its somewhat fantastic imagery. It and the other passages like it are basically the Virgilian descent into hell. It might be added that in these passages the phrases descriptive of hell are frequently very close to those in Sackville's *Induction.*

Along with the figurative journey, Hieronimo, in similar passages, may draw in other details from the medieval poems; and the journey itself may become highly disguised:

Where shall I run to breath abroad my woes . . .?
The blustring winds, conspiring with my words,
At my lament haue moued the leaueles trees,
Disroabde the medowes of their flowred greene . . .
Yet still tormented is my tortured soule
With broken sighes and restles passions,
That winged mount, and, houering in the aire,
Beat at the windowes of the brightest heauens,
Solliciting for iustice and reuenge.
But they are plac't in those empyreal heights,
Where, countermurde with walles of diamond,
I find the place impregnable, and they
Resist my woes, and giue my words no way.

(III, 7, 1 ff.)

For this complaint Kyd seems to have picked up phrases and images from the Virgil-Sackville stream of literature. He uses the connection of a natural aspect with a state of mind, repeating the diction of Sackville: *blustering winds, leafless trees, disrobed meadows, flowered green*—no collection of words could do more to reproduce the tone of the beginning of Sackville's *Induction*, and this is also to echo the beginnings of many medieval allegorical poems, including Gavin Douglas' Prologue to Book VII of the *Aeneid*, the immediate source of Sackville's lines. The latter part of the passage is plainly a variation on the Virgilian descent into hell, for the central description that the place is "countermurde with walles of diamond" and impregnable is practically borrowed from Kyd's own description of hell (". . . the faire Elizian greene, In midst whereof there stands a stately Towre, The walles of brasse, the gates of adamant." Induction to the *S. T.*)

and is extremely close to Virgil's Tartarus. We know too that it is to hell that Hieronimo habitually promises to go in search of justice and revenge. And the sighs and passions which mount, winged, hovering in the air, have a resemblance to Virgil's unborn spirits. It is the imagery of the Virgilian and medieval hell which Kyd applies to heaven. In more than one way, Kyd deserved the jibe of Nashe for the liberties he took with the location of Elysium.

The use of the materials of the tragedies and the journeys for the metaphorical language in which Horatio's parents express their grief, provided, thus, the necessary imagery upon which effective expression of such feelings depends, and it also provided the perhaps even more valuable movement, the longer harmonies, which are essential to the best dramatic blank verse. Each of the speeches in which Hieronimo swears that he will go down into hell in search of justice and revenge develops an intensity which mounts from line to line. Or some lines of Isabella—no doubt a further variation on the metaphorical journey into hell—will illustrate what I mean:

> My soule—poore soule, thou talkes of things
> Thou knowst not what—my soule hath siluer wings,
> That mounts me up vnto the highest heauens—
> To heauen: I, there sits my *Horatio*,
> Backt with a troup of fiery Cherubins
> Dauncing about his newly healed wounds,
> Singing sweet hymnes and chanting heauenly notes . . .
> (III, 8, 14 ff.)

Intensity, vigor, and movement are apparent here. In comparison with the studied, witty, euphuistic lines of earlier poets, these lines are simple and ringing; in comparison with the broad ringing heroics of the earlier Marlowe, they are sensitive, complex, and deeply motivated. In mechanics, so far as analysis can show, they are much the same as similar lines of Shakespeare.

Indeed it seems that Kyd, in these passages, is laying the foundation for Shakespeare's energetic, figurative poetry, the poetry in which joy or anguish of spirit expresses itself. On the side of mental anguish we might look at such lines as these of Macbeth:

> —Now o'er the one half-world
> Nature seems dead, and wicked dreams abuse
> The curtain'd sleep; witchcraft celebrates
> Pale Hecate's offerings; and wither'd murder,
> Alarum'd by his sentinel, the wolf,
> Whose howl's his watch, thus with his stealthy pace,
> With Tarquin's ravishing strides, toward his design
> Moves like a ghost.

Shakespeare, in making Macbeth speak thus in hysterical tones, gathers together in a single collection most of the images to which our attention has been directed. There are the semi-personifications *dreams* and *sleep*—*dreams* are regularly personified in medieval literature, and *sleep* is one of Sackville's allegorical figures at the mouth of hell. There is mention of Hecate, who, as other parts of the play show, comes from an infernal region exactly like the one Kyd describes. The complete personification *withered murder* suggests the portraits done by Sackville and the allegorists. Tarquin has come probably from Shakespeare's own modified metrical tragedy, *Lucrece*, to do metaphorical duty here. In close conjunction with the references to dreams, to an infernal creature, and to a typically medieval personification, there is the image of the ghost. Such fusion of material and such adapting of material to the purposes of drama constitute in all likelihood a debt which English dramatists owe to Thomas Kyd.

For Kyd took features of the Virgilian descent into hell and made of them the language of Hieronimo's suffering. An important step in this direction had already been made by Sackville in his *Induction*, for Sackville linked the descent into hell with a vision growing out of extreme sorrow, and even earlier poets did almost the same thing. But Kyd changed this from a narrative to a vehicle for expressing emotion; he provided the imagery necessary for a metaphorical journey of the troubled spirit. Hieronimo's agony is the core of *The Spanish Tragedy;* it is expressed almost entirely in the terms we have examined. Those same terms very soon became the language of the most intense parts of new and greater plays.

And to say that at last there is perfected here the language of suffering is to say that suffering has become articulate. Articulation goes hand in hand with ultimate understanding and adjustment; and understanding and adjustment, though they do not prevent the fates, though they see only death before them, are nevertheless the soul of tragedy.

CHAPTER III

THE SPANISH TRAGEDY, TITUS ANDRONICUS AND SENECANISM

IN BEGINNING the last chapter we proposed that a historical account of the tragic medium ought to be very much like an epitome of the history of tragedy. English tragedy, accordingly, would appear to have the four or five important historical elements at which we have been looking: the popular element, the purely ranting strain which the dramatists in general inherited from the old religious drama; the satiric moral elements, inherited mainly from the old alliterative poetry; the oratorical element which, in the drama of Peele and Marlowe and Shakespeare, develops from the stately speeches of *Gorboduc* into passionate expositions spoken by tragic protagonists; and finally the medieval versions of classical elements—the epical manner, inspired particularly perhaps by Lucan, which extends from Grimald into the works of Kyd and Marlowe, and the Virgilian element which begins with Douglas and runs through Surrey and Sackville to become, in part, the metaphorical instrument of Kyd and Shakespeare. This, I think, is a sound preliminary sketch of the fundamental continuities in our subject.

But English tragedy is of course much more complicated in its origins and development than this sketch indicates. The most important structural characteristics of the tragic form are not indicated. This is the subject to which we must now turn. We can begin best with an investigation of the external structure of *The Spanish Tragedy;* and after showing how insufficient is the hypothetical influence of Seneca and how vital is the influence of native poetical forms, we can proceed to an analysis of *Titus Andronicus*, and to some solution of the problem of Senecan influence in general.

PART I [1]

I.

It is a commonplace that Thomas Kyd, in his *Spanish Tragedy*, established upon the popular Elizabethan stage the tragedy of blood, with the peculiar violence which characterizes it, the sensational rhetoric, the revenge theme, and the ghost. These features of Kyd's drama, together with the five acts and choruses, have long been thought derived from the Senecan tragedies. We have already seen something of Kyd's rhetoric, and shall touch upon it again later on. The proposals of Senecan origins, however, for the most conspicuous features of Kyd's drama—the Ghost of Andrea and his allegoric companion, Revenge, who together form the chorus of the tragedy—are even more qualified to provoke a normal skepticism. These are matters which should be worked out coolly and carefully, and from the ground up.

J. A. Symonds, in his *Shakespeare's Predecessors*,

first pronounced the Ghost an importation from Seneca. Symonds' pronouncement became a central principle in J. W. Cunliffe's extraordinarily influential work on Seneca's influence;[2] and a few years later F. S. Boas wrote that the appearance of the Ghost and Revenge "is suggested by the opening of Seneca's *Thyestes*."[3] More recently F. L. Lucas has strongly implied, at least, that these two creations are modeled on Seneca.[4] And one of the latest commentators, T. S. Eliot, says definitely that they "replace the Tantalus and the Fury of the *Thyestes*."[5] Meanwhile the Senecan theory had been adopted by most of the general handbooks.

The consensus of scholarly opinion will be found to contain, at times ambiguously, two distinct propositions: (1) Kyd's use of the chorus is Senecan; (2) the figures which compose the chorus—one of them or both—are Senecan. We may reserve comment on the first proposition until later. The second proposition, however, is entirely unconvincing, for ghosts are essential to medieval traditions in tragedy, and personifications like Revenge are quite exclusively medieval. Kyd's use, furthermore, of an *induction* immediately suggests some connection with earlier nondramatic poetry. And finally, whatever the virtues or weaknesses of the argument that Senecan creations are models for Kyd's Ghost and Revenge, it is only an argument by analogy. The analogy, moreover, is one upon which the most cautious scholars have insisted with no great degree of severity; Cunliffe for instance, sums up his remarks on Kyd's play by saying that distinctive features of Seneca's mode of treatment are wanting.

Our present attack on the subject aims to present what seems to be a more convincing analogy; it maintains that the Ghost of Andrea and Revenge are adaptations of stock characters in the medieval metrical "tragedies." It holds that the Ghost is a variation on the ghosts who, in the metrical tragedies, come back to this world to recount their "falls"; that Revenge is one of the supernatural beings of medieval literature who act as guides, interpreters, and interlocutors, in the "marvelous journeys"—journeys which might be like that of a ghost back into the world. It recognizes that *The Spanish Tragedy* is more than a dramatization of the metrical tragedy in its narrowest form, that is, more than a dramatized recital of Andrea's unhappy death; but it argues that certain popular "tragedies" were likely to pay more attention to embellishments of ghosts and guides and marvelous journeys—features of Kyd's dramatic machinery—than to Chaucer's "certain story" of him that is

> y-fallen out of heigh degree
> Into miserie, and endeth wrecchedly;

and that Kyd's adaptation of tragical machinery is quite in line with earlier adaptations.

These proposals, it is doubtless apparent, rest on the assumption which is usual to this study, that Kyd in constructing a drama may have been influenced by nondramatic poetry. In *The Spanish Tragedy*, however, nondramatic poetical elements have long been recognized. Dr. F. S. Boas noted the "superfluity of narrative" and the "epic material" in the first act; [6] he also pointed out, in connection with the Induction, that a "greater than Seneca stood in part sponsor to the play," that is, Virgil; and that the larger part of this Induction is modeled on the *Aeneid*, VI.[7] The present intention is to pursue the implications of Dr. Boas' observations, to emphasize the Virgilian rather than the Senecan element.

2.

Ample and striking precedent for a ghost like Andrea, for a personification like his companion, Revenge, and for the events with which these two are associated, is to be found even in so well known a collection of "tragedies" as *The Mirror for Magistrates.* Thomas Sackville's contribution, for instance, contains a famous *Induction* in which a personification acts as guide for a marvelous journey, and also a vengeful ghost. An analysis of Sackville's *Induction* and his *Complaint of Buckingham*, with some notes on the work of his contemporaries and predecessors in the field of metrical tragedy, will throw a rather better light, I think, on the most important features of Kyd's drama.

Sackville's *Induction* is a poem introductory to his "tragedy" of Buckingham, and was intended as an introduction to a series of tragedies. It provides an artistic framework which would hold together, and make dramatic, the narratives of "falls." Interest in such artistic *cadre* was traditional; the ordinary procedure was to have the ghosts of the fallen Worthies appear successively, as in a vision, before the poet. This had already occurred in Boccaccio, and in Lydgate's *Fall of Princes,* and also in Lyndsay's *Tragedie of the Late Cardinal;* it became a characteristic device in *The Mirror.* The ghost, moreover, was sometimes conducted from the infernal regions to the poet's chamber, to the "stage," by a guide; such a guide in the *Fall of Princes,* Book VI, is Fortune; in Higgins' contribution to *The Mirror* it is Morpheus. For a ghost and guide to make an ascent from hell, it should be held in mind, is one of the fundamental devices of the metrical tragedy.

The *Induction* of Sackville, however, is a narrative of a descent into hell. It follows a conventional medieval form, the "marvelous journey." The poet finds himself in a somber landscape; his mind is busy with the mutability of things, and particularly with the "fall of peers." In his daze there appears to him a supernatural being—Sorrow, a personification of his own feelings—as an objectification of the keynote of the events which are about to take place. This being, acting as guide and interpreter, conducts the poet into the realm of the dead, where he hears the ghost of Buckingham recount the story of his "fall."

This narrative, it will be observed, modifies conventional "tragical" machinery in that, instead of the ghosts' being guided into the presence of Sackville,

Sackville is guided into the realm of ghosts. But it is no long leap from the conventional; it simply marks a final fusion of "marvelous journey" and "tragedy." The journey of the *Induction* is parallel with that of Lyndsay's *Dreme*, in which Lyndsay, guided into hell by Dame Remembrance, describes in detail the bad princes and ecclesiastics whom he beheld, but does not dwell on their individual "tragical" stories. Higgins, too, in *The Mirror* of 1575, uses elements of the marvelous journey; after introducing Morpheus in an "Induction," he makes Morpheus act as his guide for the journey to the place where the ghosts are to appear, to act as interpreter in their conversations about the ghosts, and also to present the ghosts to him.

While holding his *Induction* in line with traditional medieval poetry, Sackville was also under the influence of Virgil. This has been commonly recognized; it is important here because Kyd, in his "Induction," as Dr. Boas pointed out, also echoed Virgil. Both Inductions are modeled on Book VI of the *Aeneid*. Sackville's guide, Sorrow, replaces Aeneas' guide, the Sibyl; Sackville's description of the allegoric personages within the gates of hell, as well as his notes on the geography and scenery of hell, springs from Virgil. These matters, like the notes on the habitat of Sorrow —"among the Furies in the infernal lake," etc.—are things which are likely, when they occur in the drama, to be called Senecan; they are often Virgilian.

Here in this dark Virgilian hell, the ghost of Buckingham recites his "tragedy." *The Complaint of Buck-*

ingham, in most respects, is quite like the regular metrical tragedies. Buckingham tells how he aided Richard III in crime; and how, after he had rebelled against Richard, he was betrayed into his hands. This account is interspersed with moralizings proper to tragedies, and Buckingham goes so far as to say that his fall was deserved. And yet the central theme in Buckingham's account is a most passionate demand for vengeance.

The climax of the piece is a violent imprecation against the man who made known his place of hiding to Richard III. Buckingham, after he has swooned at the memory of his betrayal, cries out:

> Thou, *Banastair*, gainst thee I clepe and call
> Unto the gods, that they iust vengeaunce take
> On thee, thy bloud, thy stayned stocke and all . . .[8]

He goes on to pray that one of his betrayer's sons may die insane in a pigsty, that the other be drowned in a puddle of water, that his daughter become abhorrent with leprosy. This imprecation extends through fourteen stanzas; another fifteen stanzas are introduction and conclusion to it; and there are but one hundred and eleven stanzas in the whole poem.[9]

Whatever the connections with the classics may be, ghosts, revenge, and allegoric figures—the features of Kyd's drama—were thoroughly imbedded in English literature well before Kyd's day.

3.

It seems best to state now in bald terms the parallelism in the Ghost-Revenge machinery of *The Spanish*

Tragedy and the machinery of the embellished metrical tragedy. Revenge is a variation on the traditional guide and interpreter of the "marvelous journey." He is parallel with Sackville's Sorrow and with Virgil's Sibyl. He is unlike these in that he is guide for a ghost; in this respect, however, he is like the guides of the metrical tragedies, like the personification, Fortune, who guided certain ghosts to Lydgate; [10] or, in *The Mirror*, like Morpheus who guided from hell the ghosts which provide the whole first group of tragedies. A figure like Revenge is the natural result of the fusion of metrical tragedy and marvelous journey.

The Ghost is primarily an adventurer on a marvelous journey; he is led by a guide into a strange realm where he sees extraordinary events. His appearance with a guide on a "stage" was, of course, conventional in the metrical tragedies; but, though a return to the realm of the living is obviously a marvelous journey for the ghost, Kyd seems to be the first writer to stress the ghost's wonderment at what he sees. The Ghost's ancient rôle in the metrical tragedies—that of recounting his "fall"—is reduced to a few lines at the beginning of the play.

From the point of view of the Ghost, the central action of Kyd's drama provides the wondrous events which adventurers on miraculous journeys always beheld; and at the same time these events, in that they represent the downfall of princes, constitute a "tragedy." The Ghost, in the rôle of witness to events of a marvelous journey, does just what such witnesses always did: he tells a narrative of a journey through conventional scenes—the same scenes, in fact, as those of Sackville's *Induction.* He becomes an amazed spectator of happenings in a realm completely different from his own. In these happenings he can foresee nothing; he shows no inclinations towards vengeance until, late in the play, he sees his friend murdered and his enemies flaunting their prosperity. The Ghost proves himself the most curious member of the audience. He is as much in need of a guide and interpreter as were all the other amazed witnesses to events of a marvelous journey.

There are, furthermore, within the body of the play, some very significant references to ghosts. The father and mother of Horatio, as the anguish at the murder of their son deepens upon them, begin to see visions in which the central figure is the ghost of the murdered Horatio. Isabella exclaims at one point:

> See, where his Ghoast solicites with his wounds
> Reuenge on her that should reuenge his death.
> *Hieronimo,* make haste to see thy sonne,
> For sorrow and dispaire hath scited me
> To heare *Horatio* plead with *Radamant.*[11]

Isabella is saying figuratively that she is going to die. But she also says that she is going on a marvelous journey and that Sorrow and Despair will be her guides. In other words, Kyd reproduces here the outline of a poem like Sackville's *Induction*—in which Sorrow is also the guide for the marvelous journey—in the form of a figure of speech. Moreover, in *The Mirror*, the ghosts always appear as they do above—soliciting with their wounds, asking for notice of their deaths. And the foregoing passage, like several others in the play, shows conclusively that ghosts, guides, and personifications were inextricably bound together in Kyd's mind.

Seneca's treatment of ghosts, except for surface similarities, is entirely different from this of Kyd. Two parallels to Kyd occur in Seneca's *Agamemnon*, in which "Thyestis umbra" opens the play, and in his *Thyestes*, in which the first scene is shared between "Umbra Tantali" and Magaera. These ghosts are prologues who drop out of the play at the end of the scene, although Thyestes' influence might be said to hang over the whole of *Agamemnon;* as prologues they give information necessary for the understanding of the play and foreshadow its end. They are not the chorus. Kyd's Ghost is both a great deal more and a great deal less than a prologue. He is more, for he remains on the stage throughout the play, and he acts the rôle of the chief, and the most amazed, spectator of the action. He is less than a prologue, for he can give no information about the central action and cannot foresee its end; and it is not his influence that hangs over the tragedy, but that of Revenge. As for the function of the Ghost and Revenge as a chorus, it is fundamentally the same as that of the connecting links between the tragedies in *The Mirror* of 1575, in which Higgins converses about the action with Morpheus; it is Senecan only in that it divides the play into five acts.

There is also a great contrast between these ghosts in regard to what they tell of their experiences after death. Andrea relates the allegorists' time-worn tale of a descent into hell—a rough outline of those of Aeneas, Lyndsay, and Sackville; he repeats the standard notes on the geography, the scenery, and the inhabitants of hell. Seneca is not interested in such a narrative.[12] Instead he mentions the horrors suffered by Tantalus, for instance, for the sake of showing in a figure the horror of the events which are about to take place, saying that the experience of Tantalus is nothing in comparison with what is going to happen. Seneca's ghosts present a series of terrible images for the single end of building up the horror of the matter which they are prologuizing. But Andrea's tale is an astonishing, almost gay, narrative. If Kyd had modeled his Ghost on Seneca, he could never have written:

> Whereat faire *Proserpine* began to smile,
> And begd that onely she might give my doome.
> *Pluto* was pleasd, and sealde it with a kisse.[13]

As for the connection of a ghost with a revenge theme—the final point in which Kyd has been judged to resemble Seneca—the real difference between the two authors lies in their dissimilar attitudes to revenge. For Seneca revenge results from a family curse of long duration; betrayal, murder, and incest in preceding generations are sources of his tragedies. And, as these sins reappear in the form of far-reaching consequences, one of the original participators in the sin is called up as an embodiment of the motivating force in the tragedy. Such are Seneca's ghosts. The ghost of Thyestes in *Agamemnon* is vengeful; but his machinations have caused the tragedy. The ghost of Tantalus is not vengeful; he is the unwilling victim of a Fury and regrets what must take place. With Kyd, on the other hand, the Ghost of Andrea, unlike Thyestes, has no responsibility for the tragedy; nor is he in any ordinary sense the victim of Revenge. Andrea, moreover, has no vengeful tendencies until he is inspired to them by the events which he is witnessing. This is of greatest significance. The revenge theme, which develops slowly in the mind of Hieronimo, develops with corresponding slowness in the mind of the Ghost. For a revenge movement to begin slowly and mount to a wild climax is foreign to Seneca, but it is the whole story of Kyd's play and the most striking characteristic of Sackville's *Buckingham*.

Thus—to summarize—*The Spanish Tragedy*, in form, stems from the metrical tragedies in that a ghost appears with a guide and begins telling a narrative of his life and death. This brief narrative completed, the Ghost immediately becomes the adventurer of the marvelous journey, the central action of the play being the events of the journey. The guide, in a fashion perfectly normal to the marvelous journey, interprets the events and personifies the underlying theme in them. Kyd's formal achievement is in simplest terms a combination of tragedy and journey.

THE INFLUENCE OF SENECA

PART II

I.

Such, then, is the external form of Kyd's *Spanish Tragedy*.

Various phases of the problem of Senecan influence on Elizabethan tragedy have already demanded considerable space in these pages. It is convenient now to look at the problem as a whole with the intention of resolving it as far as possible and of returning to it only to illuminate certain ethical matters.

However much one may be disinclined to carp, there is no way to avoid the flat statement that scholarship in this field, inadequate in itself, has led the general critic into sheer confusion. The remarks of the early editors of Shakespeare have their value; Capell's note, for instance, that the word *nuntius* argues a perusing of Seneca by the author of *Titus Andronicus*, is interesting, though I think it is a very weak argument.[14] It is valuable, in other words, to try to extend the list of books which a Shakespeare may have read and which have left their mark on the author's mind. But it is distortion to single out one book and to see its influence alone. Distortion ran wild in our subject the moment it submitted to the mechanics of the dissertation writer; the thesis that Seneca influenced Elizabethan, as well as contemporaneous French, drama wandered over into a demonstration that Seneca was an exclusively great influence on these dramas. All this happened subtly, possibly without the authors' knowledge that it was happening; it is the usual fault in the sterilely analytical sort of dissertation which studies the "influence" of one document on another.

The distortions, the misleading implications, of the special studies reappeared in the form of explicit errors on the pages of the general studies, and these in turn have caused a fairly common misapprehension of pre-Shakespearean tragedy and of Shakespeare's own art.[15] Take for example one detail from the relevant paragraphs in a standard textbook like Legouis and Cazamian's *History of English Literature:* the Senecan plays, we read, "and, above all, *Thyestes* and the horrible banquet of Atreus, led to tragedies of atrocious vengeance like *Titus Andronicus* . . ."[16] I think that this statement is erroneous; it is repeated by practically all commentators on *Andronicus.*

Since this statement is typical of Senecan criticism, and since *Andronicus* itself has obvious claims to the closest sort of kinship with Kyd's play and was mentioned by Ben Jonson along with *The Spanish Tragedy,* it is a most natural subject for discussion here. Consequently I shall attempt now to do two things at the same time: to consider both *Titus Andronicus* and the constructions of the Senecans. This plan has its attractions, for in a way to do either of the things alone is unsatisfactory. To raise exhaustive objections to Senecanism is a thankless task, and to force prominence upon a tragedy which is usually regarded as a doubtful example of Shakespeare's work is to labor upon slippery ground.[17]

2.

The theory of a connection between *Thyestes* and *Titus Andronicus* goes back, or so the footnote to Professor Legouis' paragraph seems to indicate, to an omission and a misleading implication in J. W. Cunliffe's dissertation, *The Influence of Seneca on Elizabethan Tragedy* (1893). For Professor Cunliffe, in enumerating what appeared to be Senecan features in *Andronicus*, referred to the climactic incident as, and only as, a "Thyestean banquet."[18] The intended implication is apparent; the omission consists in a failure to mention Ovid. The omission is bewildering, for in the course of the play there are six clear allusions to the real source of the banquet incident, Ovid's story of Philomel (*Metamorphoses*, Bk. VI); earlier editors like Steevens and Malone, moreover, had introduced elaborate cross references to Ovid.

To bring up *Thyestes* at all is distortion, for the horrible banquet, instead of being an isolated incident in the English play, is integrally related to other events precisely as it is in Ovid; it is specifically revenge for a rape followed by the cutting out of the victim's tongue. The further mutilation of the victim—amputation of her hands—is, according to the text, a device intended directly to prevent her from using Philomel's method of revealing the crime.

In comparison with the Philomel story, moreover, the Senecan narrative was unfamiliar. For Ovid's version of the terrible story had been retold by Gower in the *Confessio Amantis*, by Chaucer in part in *The*

Legend of Good Women, by Pettie in *A Petite Palace*, by Gascoigne in *The Complaint of Philomene*, and by Golding in five editions of his translation of the *Metamorphoses*—in these tremendously influential books as well as in Ovid's Latin original. The constant references of the song writers to the nightingale and its complaining notes, "Teru, teru," are allusions to the tale; and so are the dramatists' references to the ill-fortuned lapwing.

The disposition of the revolting feast itself is, of course, different in *Titus Andronicus* from what it is in either Ovid or Seneca, different in just the same way that the English plot taken as a whole is different from its complex and still partly undetermined sources. In *Andronicus*, for instance, Titus and Lavinia prepare the banquet; in the *Metamorphoses* Progne and Philomel make the preparations in quite the same fashion; but in *Thyestes* Atreus works alone, and the scene is accomplished by the use of a messenger and chorus. On the other hand only in *Andronicus* and *Thyestes* is the number of victims the same. Other details of the event vary in each of the three versions. But for a deflowered and peculiarly mutilated woman to assist in contriving a peculiar, gruesome vengeance—this is what connects *Andronicus* with Ovid and probably with Ovid alone.

Nevertheless the English plot-maker's heightening, in comparison with Ovid's treatment, of the gory aspects of the butchery is the sort of thing which is usually laid at Seneca's door. Emphasis on physical horror is scarcely a sure indication of Senecan influence, and in this scene the grimmest of the devices—the way in which the parent is confronted with the heads of the devoured children—springs, I believe, from another tradition. Seneca causes Atreus simply to show the heads to Thyestes and lets hysterical speeches furnish the horror. Ovid, who like all story tellers must depend more than the dramatist on highly visible details, has Philomel fling the bloody head into the face of Tereus. Titus has the heads served up in coffins or shells of pastry, a device which was possibly suggested by his bitter, and peculiarly Elizabethan, punning remembrance of the coffin in which he bore home his own sons' bodies from the wars with the Goths.[19]

But Titus' device in its essential form was already a part of the Philomel story. It had been put there by John Gower, who wrote:

> This Philomene toke the hede
> Betwene two disshes, and all wrothe
> Tho camen forth the susters bothe
> And setten it upon the bord.[20]

Now it may be or it may not be that the later plot was influenced by the *Confessio Amantis:* the question is not important. What is important is the indication that the later plot was varied and expanded along lines which were natural to John Gower, that *Andronicus* shows traits of classical-medieval narrative art. If the scene had been expanded along lines natural to Seneca the increase would have been in ranting, unstable, lurid, declamatory, but not oratorical, commentary on a situation; but since it is expanded along classical and medieval narrative lines the increase is in vivid and horrible details of action. For, though it seem a paradox, the story teller always appeals to his audience's visual imagination with a greater number of spectacular details than does the dramatist himself: there are, for example, more action and more details of action in this fairly short tale of Ovid than in a Senecan drama, and the narrative is more directly and sternly gruesome. So, indeed, is almost any metrical tragedy. Consequently I think that the peculiar horrors of the Elizabethan tragedy come, in part, from transposing narrative art directly into dramatic art.[21]

Andronicus contains still other medieval additions to the Philomel story. There is first the important rôle played by personified abstractions. Gower had introduced the tale by having the Confessor give an account of the semi-personification Ravine. And Gascoigne, transforming it into a complaint, had followed the conventions of the dream-visions and the metrical tragedies by calling up the abstraction Nemesis to act as the narrator.

> She cast sometimes, a grieuous frowning glance,
> As who would say: by this it may appeare,
> That iust reuenge, is prest for euery chance.
> In hir right hand, (which to and fro did shake)
> She bare a skourge, with many a knottie string,
> And in hir left, a snaffle Bit or brake . . .[22]

She is obviously a part of the tradition which lies behind Revenge in *The Spanish Tragedy*. Though *Titus Andronicus* uses no such framework, it employs three feigned personifications, Revenge, Murder, and Rape, to accomplish its crucial scene (V, 2); that is, Tamora, knowing that Titus in his distraction has been calling on Revenge for aid, disguises herself and her sons and undertakes the part of the supernatural being in order to tempt him into betraying himself. The figure of Revenge seems to have here ultimate associations with Virgil's Sibyl; it is certain that only the practices of medieval poets including Sackville in the *Induction* can be regarded as foundational to this scene.

Gower also adds madness to the tale. Though as we have seen he is not uninclined towards graphic details of action, his gentle soul apparently forbids his saying that these horrible things were done by sane people. Ovid is content to say that Progne was enraged when she first marked Itys as the vehicle for her vengeance, that her rage gave way to mother-love, but that, remembering the crime against Philomel, she slew the child without a change of face. Gower has no heart for such cold-blooded vengeance; he slides over the long, horrible passage with the lines:

> Thus she that was as who saith mad
> Of wo, which hath her overlad,
> Without insight of moderhede
> Foryat pite and loste drede
> And in her chambre prively
> This childe without noise or cry
> She slough and hewe him all to pieces.
>
> (p. 287)

This tendency to hang a cloak of madness over deeds of desperate violence lends a kind of imperfect intelligibility to the slaughter at the end of *The Spanish Tragedy* and, in this play, to Titus' slaying of Lavinia. The device is imperfect; madness in these dramas actually adds to the horror. The slaughter itself, moreover, is the outcome of other conventions, both ethical and artistic.[23]

But the madness of Titus is also feigned; he simulates in order to allay the suspicions of his enemies and to contrive his triumph over them. So, too, did Progne in Ovid's story of Philomel. When Progne learned that her sister had been foully assaulted, "though malice made hir venging hart to swell," says Gascoigne, she deferred the deed "til time and place might serue." She used the Bacchic frenzies as a device forcibly to deliver Philomel from imprisonment and to bring her disguised, and amazed at the frantic actions and disguises of the others, into the house of Tereus: Progne, Ovid explains, terrific in her own rage, mimicked the madness of Bacchus. There is, in other words, method in this madness, and the madness itself is ambiguous. In comparison with it the madness of a Senecan character, of a Hercules or a Medea, is direct and unambiguous; so too, to a lesser degree, is Hieronimo's distraction. Was Progne, was Titus really mad? The answer must be, in the trite phrase, yes and no. The same ambiguity must be implicit in the Hamlet situation.[24] And, whatever may have been Shakespeare's instincts towards clarification, it is unlikely that it occurred to him to try deliberately to resolve a historically ambiguous conjunction of circumstances. For methodical madness *is* the Hamlet situation.

The mode of expression, however, the metaphor in which Titus gives vent to his affliction is that of Hieronimo through and through; it is that reduction of features of marvelous journeys to a metaphorical journey of a troubled spirit which was a topic of discussion in the preceding chapter. In a typical outburst Hieronimo says, for instance,

> Away, Ile rip the bowels of the earth
> (*He diggeth with his dagger.*)
> And Ferrie ouer to th' Elizian plaines,
> And bring my Sonne to shew his deadly wounds.
> (III, 12, 71 ff.)

And Titus no less typically:

> Publius and Sempronius, you must do it;
> 'Tis you must dig with mattock and with spade,
> And pierce the inmost centre of the earth:
> Then, when you come to Pluto's region,
> I pray you, deliver him this petition.
> (IV, 3, 10 ff.)

Hieronimo, at another place:

> Ile downe to hell, and in this passion
> Knock at the dismall gates of *Plutos* Court,
> Getting by force, as once *Alcides* did,
> A troupe of furies and tormenting hagges,
> To torture *Don Lorenzo* and the rest.
> (III, 13, 109 ff.)

And in his fury Hieronimo tears up the petitions which

he in his capacity as civil justice has just received. Titus, not content with his own petitions to Pluto, exclaims:

> I'll dive into the burning lake below,
> And pull her [Revenge] out of Acheron by the heels . . .
> And sith there's no justice in earth or hell,
> We will solicit heaven and move the gods
> To send down Justice for to wreak our wrongs.[25]
> (IV, 3, 43 ff.)

These speeches of Titus and others as well also have interesting likenesses to the passages from *The Spanish Tragedy* which are reproduced in the foregoing chapter.

Even the device of having Hieronimo mistake the Old Man for a supernatural emissary recurs with the slightest of modifications in *Andronicus:*

> *Titus.* Why, didst thou not come from heaven?
> *Clown.* From heaven! alas! sir, I never came there. God forbid I should be so bold to press to heaven in my young days. Why, I am going with my pigeons to the tribunal plebs, to take up a matter of brawl betwixt my uncle and one of the emperial's men.
> (IV, 3, 87 ff.)

Both the Old Man and the Clown, moreover, are foils to Hieronimo and Titus in that both of the former, like the latter, are entangled in matters which call for court action. Now the lines of the Clown above have been taken by Stoll in the *Tudor Shakespeare*, as by Swinburne originally, to be evidence of Shakespeare's hand in *Andronicus*. In this judgment I agree with Professor Stoll, for the Clown is one of those marvelously pleasant bumpkins, which are only to be found in Shakespeare's earlier dramas. But the scene as a whole is thickly overshadowed by Kyd, the only noteworthy change being really the substitution of this bright and potentially poignant clown (Cf. the Fool in *Lear*) for Kyd's strictly lugubrious old man. The whole scene is possibly Shakespeare's; Shakespeare could have known how to lean on his predecessors. That he was not content to lean too heavily, the Clown indicates here; the complexity of his later dependence and independence seems to become very clear if the dialogue,

> *Polonius*. Do you know me, my lord?
> *Hamlet*. Excellent well; you are a fishmonger,
> (II, 2, 173–4)

is compared with the dialogue above. Polonius is a more canny fool, and there is more method in Hamlet's madness.

3.

These are some of the interesting features of *Titus Andronicus*. The tragedy in terms of what it really is, a transitional piece, namely, that stands between *The Spanish Tragedy* and *Hamlet*, is to be understood as (and only as, I think) a purely Elizabethan transformation of the Philomela story. It is transformed, just as are the comedies, by the addition of similar or related plot-fragments from the much favored stories of Virginia, of Lucrece, and of Coriolanus, all of which are alluded to by the text itself.[26] It derives many a rhetorical flourish directly or indirectly from Virgil. It is motivated—crudely motivated, it is true—by the wickedness of Aaron, who is only too apparently a Vice from the moral plays, a fellow with Ambidexter in *Cambyses,* with Vulluppo and Lorenzo in *The Spanish Tragedy,* with Ithamore and Muly Mahamet—who nevertheless displays in his love for his little black bastard son a redeeming, and stirringly Gothic, mixture of qualities and is potentially therefore not incomparable with Iago. The motivation is faulty, in fact, not so much because of the rôle played by Aaron as because Aaron is too easily successful in the rôle: Titus, unlike Othello, does not have sufficient inherent powers for opposing overwhelming wickedness. As for the comparison of *Andronicus* with *Hamlet,* the essential difference, and it is a great difference, is that the treatment of character in the former, even beside Kyd's model, stays far too much on the surface, is exterior and unconvincing, while in the latter, along with other refinements, the treatment is superbly interior.

In this account Seneca's name does not appear. As a matter of fact even the findings of the Senecan specialists are fairly vague, confined either to very broad general principles or to minor "reminiscent" passages. One such passage constitutes the topic for the most imposing part of Professor Cunliffe's discussion of *Andronicus;* it is introduced as follows:

The description of the "barren detested vale," the scene of the murder of Bassianus and the rape of Lavinia, reminds us of the place where Atreus sacrificed his nephews.[27]

The passage, if we reassemble it, is this:

> The trees, though summer, yet forlorn and lean,
> O'ercome with moss and baleful mistletoe:
> Here never shines the sun; here nothing breeds,
> Unless the nightly owl or fatal raven:
> And when they show'd me this abhorred pit,
> They told me, here, at dead time of the night,
> A thousand fiends, a thousand hissing snakes,
> Ten thousand swelling toads, as many urchins,
> Would make such fearful and confused cries,
> As any mortal body hearing it
> Should straight fall mad, or else die suddenly.
>
> (II, 3, 94 ff.)

Beside these lines Professor Cunliffe puts *Thyestes* 650–5 and 668–673; and beside line four, *Hercules Furens* 690–2. What sense, or really how little sense, or what vaguely obscure sense Elizabethans found in the first of the suggested passages appears in Jasper Heywood's translation:

> The privie Palaice underlieth
> in secret place aloe,
> With ditch ful deepe that doth enclose
> the wood of privitee,
> And hidden parts of kyngdome olde:
> where never grew no tree
> That chereful bowes is woont to beare,
> with knife or lopped be,
> But Tare, and Cypresse, and with tree
> of Holme ful blacke to see
> Doth becke and bende the wood so darke . . .
>
> (Newton's *Seneca*, I, 78)

The other passage from *Thyestes* is thick with ghosts, of which there is none in the lines from *Andronicus*, and is lacking in fiends, snakes, toads, and urchins.

But the barren detested vale should never have reminded us of *Thyestes* in the first place. It could do so only if we had an unfortunate *idée fixe* about a Thyestean banquet, in which we were determined to persevere with willful blindness. For the text instructs us on the point with more patience and clarity than biased readers deserve:

Titus.
Lavinia, wert thou thus surpris'd, sweet girl,
Ravish'd and wrong'd, as Philomela was,
Forc'd in the ruthless, vast, and gloomy woods?
See, see!
Ay, such a place there is, where we did hunt,—
O! had we never, never hunted there,—
Pattern'd by that the poet here describes,
By nature made for murders and for rapes.
(IV, 1, 51 ff.)

The lines in question are elaborated from Ovid's

. . . cum rex Pandione natam
in stabula alta trahit, silvis obscura vetustis.[28]

And it would be scarcely reasonable to suppose that, for suggestions in elaborating so common a subject, a poet who displays in *The Rape of Lucrece* a miraculous power for making variations on the theme of gloom and night, or who in *A Midsummer Night's Dream*, say, puts the terrors of the woods into terms ranging from the song "You spotted snakes . . ." with its allusion to Philomel, to the wormy beds of the damned spirits that "in cross-ways and floods have burial" (III, 2, 383)—that this poet, given the situation, would have to seek stimulation in any text whatsoever. If there is doubt about this, look again at the passage; the juxtaposition of summer and the lean trees, the owl and the raven, the fiends, snakes, toads, and urchins —these, it seems to me, come steaming from the witches' pot of the Shakespearean imagination. Or if they are denied the honor of being Shakespeare's, any Elizabethan poet could hardly have failed to make his own independent elaboration of this sort of material.

The same things must be said about the hunting scenes, which also bulk large in Cunliffe's account of Senecan influence on this tragedy. "The description of rural life and scenery," writes Cunliffe, "which relieve the sanguinary picture to some extent, are not strange to Seneca. The hunting scene (II, 2) might be suggested by the opening of the *Hippolytus*, and the lines in II, 3:—

> The birds chant melody on every bush;
> The snake lies rolled in the cheerful sun;
> The green leaves quiver with the cooling wind,

may be compared with *Hippolytus* 516–8 . . ."[29] Note first of all the method in which this criticism is founded: the critic finds a hunting scene in *Andronicus;* since he is in search only of Senecan influences, he asks himself where hunting scenes occur in Seneca; the answer is obvious, in *Hippolytus*. And there, with an urbane suggestion as to the comparison, the critic stops. What marvels such a sovereign method could be capable of!

And if it is necessary to exhibit the confusions inherent in such a method, we need only restore the lines above to their context:

> The birds chant melody on every bush,
> The snake lies rolled in the cheerful sun,
> The green leaves quiver with the cooling wind,
> And make a chequer'd shadow on the ground.
> Under their sweet shade, Aaron, let us sit,
> And, whilst the babbling echo mocks the hounds,
> Replying shrilly to the well-tun'd horns,
> As if a double hunt were heard at once,
> Let us sit down and mark their yelping noise;
> And after conflict, such as was suppos'd,
> The wandering prince and Dido once enjoy'd . . .
> (II, 3, 12–22)

What should have been the critic's first hypothesis is proved here: that, namely, the poet associated his hunting scene, not with *Hippolytus*, but with the most famous of hunting scenes in literature. With so much certain, the inference must follow that the scene is independent or at least a very complex development of the Virgilian scene, just as Chaucer's indescribably brilliant development of the same scene in *The Legend of Good Women* is complex and, in the most real sense of the term, his own. At least the *Hippolytus* theory rests on the preliminary assumption that the earlier scene suggested the later one, and this, with a certainty that is rare in literary problems, is demonstrably false.

Finally, it would be indeed an extraordinary poet who, with the hunting scene from the *Aeneid* in mind, would have to borrow his cheeping birds and quivering trees from another source, or from any source. For these commonest pieces of common poetic property are all that Seneca has to offer:

> Hic aves querulae fremunt,
> ramique ventis lene percussi tremunt,
> veteresque fagi.[30]

The poetry, moreover, of these hunting scenes in *Andronicus* (II, 2 and II, 3) is so genuinely like that of *Venus and Adonis* that it is considerable evidence of the Shakespearean authorship of the tragedy. Compare, for instance, the lines in the passage above,

> . . . whilst the babbling echo mocks the hounds,
> Replying shrilly to the well-tun'd horns,
> As if a double hunt were heard at once,

with *Venus and Adonis* 695–6:

> Then do they [the hounds] spend their mouths:
> Echo replies,
> As if another chase were in the skies.

This is no reminiscence of cheeping birds and quivering trees; this is a reproduction of an exceedingly complicated and unusually imaginative idea. There are only two probabilities to account for its appearance in *Andronicus:* the one, that Shakespeare has continued in his own idiom; the other, that a later poet borrowed it from *Venus and Adonis*. Of these the latter is unlikely in that a practical dramatist would scarcely be patient enough, or even capable enough, deliberately to impose such subtle changes upon a delicate and evasive idea, to perform this feat when he is in the midst of a running descriptive context: borrowing generally consists in the reproduction of forthright, unsubtle ideas or else in the direct lifting of rhythmic structures.

Besides, when this out-of-doors poetry first enters *Andronicus*, it not only recapitulates *Venus and Adonis* in spirit and vocabulary but it merges immediately into something else, something which is a primary characteristic of Shakespearean construction—a tragic premonition woven tightly into the larger fabric. It is Titus who introduces the scene:

> The hunt is up, the morn is bright and grey . . .
>
> (II, 2, 1)

And Titus who eight lines farther on is saying:

> I have been troubled in my sleep this night,
> But dawning day new comfort hath inspir'd.

With this might be compared, of course, almost as many similar passages as there are Shakespearean tragedies, and, in view of chronology, Romeo's dream, which made his mind misgive that

> Some consequence yet hanging in the stars
> Shall bitterly begin his fearful date
> With this night's revels,
>
> (I, 4, 108 ff.)

is especially interesting. But it is even more to the point that premonitions of evil figured with extraordinary richness in the presentation of Venus.

In other words Professor Cunliffe brings up Seneca where the text itself asserts the prior claims of other traditions. And with unmistakable evidence at hand it is not difficult to see how the hunting scenes got into the tragedy. The author, intending to throw the Philomel story into an enlarged dramatic form, had to let the virtuous Lavinia fall into the power of totally wicked opponents (moral play traditions demanded modified Vices, or at least made characters so mixed as Tereus impracticable for this rôle) and be overcome, or so the text suggested, in a woodland scene. To this end a hunt was the most natural of devices, a device utilized similarly in fact by innumerable medieval romances. But a royal hunt—and the "royal" or imperial nature of these events was predicated by Elizabethan conceptions of tragedy—could not have failed to associate itself first of all and most specifically with the *Aeneid;* and this furnished grounds for revealing the relations between Tamora, the lustful queen, and Aaron. The order in which the details of the situation were worked out may have been otherwise, but this is its essential structure. With such a structure to develop, it would have been unnatural for Shakespeare not to have echoed *Venus and Adonis*, and, of course, not impossible though less natural for another poet to have done so. And so the argument comes to this: proceeding from Ovid and Virgil, who in their own right were eminently suggestive to Elizabethans and who are specified by this text, would not preclude by any means Shakespeare's continuing in his established poetic practices; but, because of the difficulty in looking in several directions at once, it makes the proposition that another poet was imitating Shakespeare improbable, and it does definitely preclude all thought of Senecan influence.

Cunliffe adduces only two more reminiscent passages. These, I believe, resemble Seneca only in that they contain some classical and medieval stereotypes of phraseology. But they also contain more than that. The one,

> Andronicus, stain not thy tomb with blood:
> Wilt thou draw near the nature of the gods?
> Draw near them then in being merciful;
> Sweet mercy is nobility's true badge,
>
> (I, 1, 116 ff.)

is interesting to all students because it is Portia's address, "The quality of mercy . . ." in little.

> And earthly power doth then show likest God's
> When mercy seasons justice.
>
> (*M. of V.*, IV, 1, 184 ff.)

Though it would be amusing to discover that generations of elocutionists have been unconscious Senecans, or Senecans by one degree removed, I am dubious. What Seneca says amounts to this: "Why shed blood? Tyrannical power does not endure, but moderation breeds strength. Only he is secure who scorns power." (Cf. *Troades* 258 ff.). The difference is great. The other passage (I, 1, 157–64) is likewise distinctively Shakespearean; it is one of the seven passages which

Sir Edmund Chambers thinks may possibly point to Shakespeare's authorship of the play.

Titus Andronicus is remarkable for the number and the baldness of its literary allusions. This in itself is characteristic of the early English tragedy, and so far as Shakespeare's early work is concerned, if we remember that this is a Roman, or perhaps better an Elizabethan classical, tragedy, the number of allusions is not surprising. However crude may be the artistic contributions of the allusions, they furnish an excellent means of reconstructing the reading of—indeed the literary influences upon—the dramatist, and of checking upon a specific problem like that of the influence of Seneca. According to my count the distribution of fairly clear classical allusions is this: Ovid, sixteen (excluding the repeated references to Philomel); Virgil, fifteen; Livy-Painter, four; Horace, two (from Lyly's grammar); Seneca, two (both are short Latin tags from *Hippolytus*); and perhaps one or two from Homer, Sophocles, Euripides, Herodotus or Plutarch, and Cicero. This list reads, both in point of names and proportionate importance, remarkably like an Elizabethan pre-university curriculum;[31] possibly it suggests as accurately as anything can the degree of the influence of Seneca on a typical author of a tragedy of blood.

PART III

In the immediately preceding pages I have been careful to consider every citation from *Titus Androni-*

cus that is contained in *The Influence of Seneca on Elizabethan Tragedy;* therefore I think that my observations are a fair indication of the fundamental insecurity in this influential work. But I hasten to make two reservations. The findings of Senecan influence in *Gismond of Salerne* and *The Misfortunes of Arthur* seem to be beyond dispute on the whole, though, of course, both plays have been shaped importantly by the source material; that is, the Italian *novella* in the former and the British legendary history in the latter. These plays are exceptional, are special, I think, somewhat in the fashion that *The Comedy of Errors* is a special phenomenon among Shakespeare's comedies.

The second reservation is tentative: it recognizes that the doctrines of the Senecans rest on general propositions which are quite unrelated to the evidence afforded by a citation of parallel passages. The generalizations comprehend both moral and technical or formal questions. Those of the former sort will be looked at later on. Those of the latter sort are our present subject.

But since questions of Senecan influence on the form of Elizabethan tragedy have received a good deal of incidental attention already, it seems necessary only to combine here in a summary fashion the substance of what has been said earlier with what still remains to be said.

1. *Five Acts.* The number of acts varies in the drama of the early sixteenth century. John Bale's comedy

Three Laws, for instance, has five acts; his "tragedy or interlude" *God's Promises* has seven acts; and his *King Johan* is broken into two acts only by dint of a revision made shortly after 1547.[32] These three plays were written in about 1538. The moral play *Respublica* (1553) is divided into five acts and into scenes as well; and of course the school comedies like *Roister Doister* and *Gammer Gurton's Nedle* employ both five acts and scenes. If *Gorboduc*, as is commonly thought (and justly, I think), regularized practice for the tragedy, it must have been upon the conventions of classical comedy rather than Senecan tragedy, for the disposition of the acts into scenes accords only with comedy; this relationship between tragedy and comedy is further testified, moreover, by the appearance of two *parasites* among the *dramatis personae*.[33] But these divisions never attained to any structural significance: the continuous, running texts of manuscripts and quartos would seem to indicate that the writers of the great Elizabethan tragedies were more interested in other structural principles.

2. *The Chorus*. The revision of Bale's *King Johan* just referred to suggests what must have been the origin of the chorus. In the manuscript of the play, which was originally continuous, a later hand entered (*c.* 1547) verses to be spoken by "the interpretour," beginning thus:

> In thys present acte, we haue to yow declared
> As in a myrrour, the begynynge of kynge Iohan . . .[34]

and ending with the notation *finit actus primus*. Now as precedent for this revision there were at least these important conventions: In the Chester Plays a *nuntius*, acting really the rôle of epilogue and prologue, presents a connecting link between "The Deluge" and "The Sacrifice of Isaac"; and after this latter pageant, as well as after the fifth and twelfth pageants, an *expositor* interprets the action and points the moral; [35] he begins—e.g.:

> Lordinges, what this may signify . . .[36]

The York Plays employ a prologue to introduce "The Annunciation" just as the Chester Plays employ a *nuntius;* dramas as different as *Everyman* and the *Four Elements* make messengers serve as prologues; and Bale himself habitually begins with *Baleus Prolocutor*. Whatever these figures may be called, they are consistently interpreters of the action; as such, they are functionally identical with the commentators who furnish connecting links in the medieval metrical tragedies, in the *Fall of Princes* as in *The Mirror for Magistrates*. As usual, Shakespeare is instructive:

> And all this dumb play had his acts made plain
> With tears, which, chorus-like, her eyes did rain.
> (*V. and A.*, 360)

And it is singly and alone as an interpreter of what has gone before (especially the symbolic material presented in the dumb shows) and what is to come afterwards that the chorus in *Gorboduc* functions. So too, in general, functions the chorus, in so far as it persists, in the later tragedy. Obviously the possible relations between the English and the Senecan practice are complicated. In *Gorboduc* the bare word *chorus* seems to go back to Seneca, though the Italians may stand in between. On the other hand Seneca's choruses are composed of people fairly intimately allied with the protagonists; the chorus of *Gorboduc*, "foure auncient and sage men of Brittaine," is composed of detached and merely symbolic figures. Seneca's choruses, similarly, rather than being strictly interpretative agents, are strictly choral adjuncts to the action; they are extensive enough to share acts with the protagonists, while English practice uses only a few pithy verses exterior to the acts; they participate in dialogue with messengers and other characters, while English custom never goes beyond its old concern with connective links. (*Gismond of Salerne* is Senecan and exceptional; *The Spanish Tragedy* is exceptional in ways which have already been described.) Structurally, then, the chorus in Elizabethan tragedy is entirely in harmony with the older and non-Senecan habits of composition: only the fact that it appears in conjunction with the generally classical scheme of five acts points to Senecan assistance in the architecture of a play like *Gorboduc*.

But after all, the chorus is even less important to English tragedy than the mechanical, five-act disposition of the scenes; and it was suppressed when two things happened—when the dramatists learned how to tell their stories naturally and easily, and when they were no longer interested in trampling down their audiences with an ironshod didacticism.

3. *The Unities.* It is amazing to find that the Senecan critics seem to accredit the Elizabethan violation of the unities of time and place to an imitation of Seneca; this, when every dramatic tradition in western Europe was not only contrary to these unities but scarcely knew there were any such things. If Elizabethan tragedy had ever approached a semblance of the unities, it might have been in imitation of Seneca; but never the contrary.

Unity of action is, of course, on one level or another a universal law in all forms of dramatic composition, and it need not be examined here.

4. *Stage Decencies.* This problem is in nature exactly like the foregoing. Cunliffe has recognized that there must be a connection between the slaying on the stage of Abel, the children of Bethlehem, Herod, and Jesus, and the bloody events enacted in *Appius and Virginia* and *Cambyses;* and that such connection is made undeniable by the intermixing of integrally related and totally un-Senecan comic material. I cannot see how anyone with these facts in mind can reject the inference that *The Spanish Tragedy* and *Titus Andronicus*, for instance, share in these conventions. And doubtless too the Elizabethans learned something about bloodshed from the metrical tragedies.

5. *The Messenger.* It is well known that when the vernacular came into the religious drama, the extra-

textual material—the speakers' names, the stage directions, etc.—remained largely in Latin. Consequently designations like *nuntius* indicate a conventional arrangement of manuscripts, and are in themselves, it would seem, an indication of non-Senecan influences.

I have already referred to the use of a *nuntius* as a prologue in the mystery plays; and I pass over the frequent incidental appearances of *nuntii* in the Cornish,[37] Towneley, Coventry, and York cycles to touch on what was doubtless the most famous and influential accomplishment of the older English drama—the staging, namely, of the story of Herod, the Magi, and the "Slaughter of the Innocents." Here, in the Coventry, Towneley, and York versions, the part of the messenger is as complete and important as it ever became in Elizabethan drama. The Coventry pageant, for instance, is held together by the rôle of the messenger, for it is a *noncios* who reports the will of Herod to the people and the Magi, and who likewise reports the movements of the Magi and the child to Herod; it is perhaps permissible to add too that the *nuntius* appears in the midst of a huge diversity of interesting stuffs—the ravings of Herod, the devotions of the Magi, the angelic apparitions, the lullabies of the mothers, the fighting between the mothers and the soldiers, and then the cutting of "thousands" of children's throats on the stage.[38] In the York play—to give another instance—a *nuntius* informs Herod that he has seen the three kings; he is told he talks too fast, and is asked whether the kings are coming to Herod's court; he says they have gone to their own countries, after having made offerings to the child and having announced that the child would be the future king of the earth; and for his news he is abused roundly by Herod and the consuls.[39]

All this is most certainly in letter and spirit the technique employed by the later dramatists, by Shakespeare in *Antony and Cleopatra* for instance. Seneca is far too sober for this sort of thing. But on the side of sobriety one might mention the moral play, the *Conflict of Conscience* (*c.* 1550), in which the account of the protagonist's death is actually limited to the report of a *nuntius*.[40] Between these extremes of liveliness and gravity the Elizabethan messenger ranges freely. He is another implement which cannot be said to have specifically this origin or that origin.

6. *The Ghost.* Ghosts, as these pages have been saying, are an essential convention in the metrical tragedies; and, if we take into account the tremendously influential works of Boccaccio, Lydgate, Lyndsay, Cavendish, Baldwin, Ferrers, Churchyard, Higgins, Blenerhasset, and Robinson, the complaining ghosts of the traditional tragedies exceed the Senecan ghosts by at least fifty to one in number and probably also in importance. And the proportion seems to continue into the tragedies written for the Elizabethan stage, for Gorlois in *The Misfortunes of Arthur* appears to be the solitary adaptation of the Senecan *umbra.* The extent to which Elizabethans clung to old customs is

clearest, however, in the very additions which Jasper Heywood entered into his translations of the Latin plays. His creation of the "Sprite of Achilles" to take an extensive part in the *Troas* has called forth this comment: "Thus, fully equipped in manner, speech, and dramatic function, the Senecan ghost first enters Elizabethan drama—and he is by law, at all events, Heywood's ghost, not Seneca's at all!" [41] More than that, he is also the ghost of the metrical tragedies: the first half of the speech given Achilles' ghost is a straightforward narrative of a fall, totally and exclusively in the manner of the medieval tragedies, and only the second half, which foretells how his vengeful desires will work themselves out, is Senecan.

And the second ghost to appear in connection with a nonmetrical tragedy, though he is not like Achilles' spirit a part of the action, is nevertheless peculiarly interesting. This is Heywood's introduction in the prologue to *Thyestes* (1560) of the ghost of Seneca himself. Heywood has been reading on a somber winter day, and when he falls asleep over his book the ghost of Seneca appears and urges him on in his project of translating the tragedies. Heywood with great modesty protests that his powers are immature, but he is finally persuaded to continue the work he had begun with the *Troas*. In adopting this machinery Heywood was far from original, or, for that matter, Senecan. In quite a similar fashion the shade of Dante appears in the Boccaccio-Lydgate tragedies and asks that the story of Duke Gaultier, an oppressor of the city of

Florence, be told.[42] In precisely the same fashion the ghost of Mapheus appears to Gavin Douglas and by dint of argument and twenty thwacking blows of his club persuades Douglas to translate the thirteenth book which Mapheus added to the *Aeneid*. Jasper Heywood, moreover, while he is protesting his humble powers to the ghost of Seneca, recommends other men who would be more suitable and capable than he—North, Sackville, Norton, and Baldwin; Baldwin—

> Whose Myrrour dothe of Magistrates,
> proclayme eternall fame.[43]

From all this two conclusions must be drawn: one, the first translator of Seneca did not distinguish between metrical tragedies and regular tragedies; the first translator, even though he had Senecan texts before him, pursued medieval conventions in part when he created the ghost of Achilles and entirely when he created the ghost of Seneca. In other words, the Senecan ghosts are only several in a large company; they doubtless encouraged the use of ghosts in the drama, but they were also probably more changed by medieval processes than they were able to change those processes.

7. *The Revenge Motive*. In utilizing a revenge motive Elizabethan writers of tragedy probably drew on a variety of precedents. Revenge is integral to such classical stories as those of Dido and Philomel; to such metrical tragedies as Boccaccio's and Lydgate's *Hannibal* and Sackville's *Buckingham;* and to the popular

modified moral plays of the sixteenth century. The latter are of special interest. The overthrow of the Vices in the late moral plays is frequently assigned to an abstract figure—to Vindicta Dei in Bale's *Three Laws,* to Divine Correction in Lyndsay's *Satyre of the Thrie Estaits,* to the Goddess Nemesis in *Respublica.* Such figures as these doubtless explain what Elizabethans had in mind when they harped on the idea of "a just revenge"; indeed Gascoigne makes the abstraction Nemesis, around whom he builds the dream-vision framework of his *Complaint of Philomene,* say that she is the instrument of just revenge, though it is a little hard to see how Gascoigne construes the justice in the events of his story; and the framework abstraction Nemesis is undoubtedly related, in convention, to Revenge in *The Spanish Tragedy.* On the other hand the Vice in the moral plays may be a personification of revenge, a personification, we may presume, of wicked revenge; this is what the Vice in *Horestes* proclaims himself in no uncertain terms, and his function is to tumble the protagonist in tragical fashion, from high estate to low. The moral significance of the revenge motive is often uncertain, but its origins in normal and familiar literature are not obscure.

8. *Rant.* In his consideration of lurid rhetoric, Cunliffe takes his text from Shakespeare. Seneca, he writes, "contents himself with amplifying the horror of the tragic situation . . . and exaggerating the expression

of passion till it becomes ridiculous. In *Hercules Furens* (1291–1301) we have an example of the style to which Nick Bottom gave the immortal title of 'Ercles' vein.' " On the surface this seems convincing: Heywood's translation of *Hercules Furens* was printed in 1561 and in 1581; and it does have its share of rant. But even so it is an exceptionally good piece of writing, too good probably for Bottom's taste; and if it was ever played upon a stage, Bottom would never have known about it. Since Shakespeare's similar characters are generally realistic in their references to the stage (cp. Pistol and Shallow), it is likely that Bottom is thinking of the non-Senecan Hercules—the Hercules of masks and interludes, to whom the old actor in Greene's *Groatsworth of Wit* (1592) is apparently referring when he says, "The twelve labors of Hercules have I terribly thundered on the stage"; the Hercules, for that matter, of *Love's Labour's Lost*, who is probably related to *Hercules Furens* in about the way that Pickering's *Horestes* is related to Seneca; that is, not at all.

But this is only one Shakespearean text, and not, it happens, a representative one. First of all should come Hamlet's remonstrances concerning robustious ranting actors who ought to be

> whipped for o'er-doing Termagant; it out-herods Herod.
> (III, 2, 15)

This characterization of rhetorical exaggeration is supported by many other references; when Mistress Page, for instance, reads Falstaff's passion-tearing lines—

Thine own true knight,
By day or night,
Or any kind of light
With all his might
For thee to fight,

(II, 1, 15)

—she can only exclaim, "What a Herod of Jewry is this!" And it is worth pointing out that the burlesque speech which Bottom declaims uses a rhyme pattern (aaabcccb) which, like Falstaff's above, is typical of the old religious drama but totally different from the fourteeners selected from the English *Hercules Furens* by the Senecan critics. Then again, when a more alert Falstaff set out to parody the ranting style, he declared he did it in "King Cambyses' vein" (1 *Hen. IV*, II, 4, 425). Never, I think, though Hercules' name, for instance, is mentioned some fifty times in the plays, does Shakespeare either name or allude to an unmistakably Senecan character, either in connection with rant or in any other connection.

9. *Sensationalism.* Fables embodying horrible events are not of course the exclusive property of Seneca but are rather a common heritage which was drawn upon by the Greeks and by the Romans including Seneca and by the Middle Ages and the sixteenth century in innumerable complicated ways. The tales which the metrical tragedies retold from history were scarcely less appallingly bloody. General sensationalism therefore is not an independent structural element in the

drama as is for instance the messenger or the ghost; it is instead a result of deep-lying causes, an effect which was cultivated because of certain attitudes towards the world. The important question is, why were Elizabethans preoccupied with sensationalism? And this question must await its place along with other moral considerations.

10. *Sententious precepts.* For centuries before Shakespeare's time writers had exercised themselves in forming impressive remonstrances on the fickleness of fortune, the cares of state, the cruelty of war, the dangers of ambition, the deceits of court life, the hazards of high place, the impetuosity of youth. . . . These subjects find expression in forms ranging from proverbs to resounding periods in state orations; from Barclay's eclogues—on the "miseries of courtiers and courts"—to Gascoigne's *Glass of Government*, a dramatization of the dangers inherent in youth. In his devotion to these subjects Seneca was one of many, and among the many from whom the dramatists borrowed.

There is serious distortion in linking the sententious precepts of the dramatists too directly with similar ones in the Senecan plays. For not only are instructive precepts to be found everywhere, but a little scrutiny shows in almost every case that the Elizabethans are uttering ideas which bear only a superficial resemblance to the Latin parallels. Two instances discussed earlier in this study are these: (1) Seneca says that a king is a law unto himself; one of the authors of *Gorboduc* says in bitter scorn that sometimes a king takes the law into his own hands; (2) Seneca has much to say about the dangers of high places and the safety of humility; Shakespeare says that mercy is a godlike attribute.[44] Parallels of this kind are false and misleading; and even when, as in *The Spanish Tragedy*, III, 1, 1 ff., lines are apparently quoted directly from Seneca, the context may still indicate only a superficial Senecanism. Consequently the whole attitude towards "commonplace" moralizing on broadly familiar subjects stands in need of revision. The likelihood is that the dramatists are expressing their own reflections on subjects which had been and were still regarded as significant, and that in so doing they are bespeaking the attitudes of their immediate age.

CHAPTER IV

TRANSFORMATIONS OF MEDIEVAL STRUCTURE: *TITUS ANDRONICUS* AND THE SHAKESPEAREAN PRACTICE

OVER AND against the structural elements in Elizabethan tragedy which have been assigned, thus insecurely, to the influence of Seneca, there are certain others which I believe are both more important in themselves and of less perplexing origins. They exerted, as will be seen, a more intimate influence on the form of tragedy than did the arrangement of five acts with choruses on the one hand or the use of such contrivances as the messenger or ghost on the other: this is merely a statement of relative importance; the five acts, chorus, messenger, and ghost are, as I think it has been shown, either historically independent of Seneca or dependent upon enormously complicated influences. The most significant of the structural principles in the great English tragedy seem to be developed fairly directly from the medieval metrical tragedy.

Most of these principles have not been without recognition and discussion; some of them have been described, but not in historical terms, in the exemplary pages of A. C. Bradley, and others have been set down in historical terms in the valuable book of Professor Willard Farnham, *The Medieval Heritage of Elizabethan Tragedy*. A large part of what I shall have to say is an extension of observations contained in these and several other works.

1. *The Pyramidal Structure.* Tragedy in the Middle Ages was the story of a great person's attainment of a special eminence, his brief and precarious triumph, and his fall. Such a story naturally took on a definite shape: its first part accounted for the ascent of the pyramid of worldly success, its second part viewed the man on the very top, and its final part ushered him down the inevitable other side: the story recapitulated in form the image of man's rise and fall upon the Wheel of Fortune.

This form is implicit and actually present more or less perfectly in the earliest *De Casibus* tragedies. In Sackville's *Buckingham* the conquest of the upward slope of the pyramid is announced in Buckingham's words concerning himself and Richard III:

> And wee aduanst to that wee bought full deare
> Hee crouned king and I his chiefest peare.
>
> (St. 27)

Here in a single breath as it were, Buckingham celebrates his triumph and predicts his downfall. The pyramidal structure is remarkably explicit, as Professor Farnham has pointed out, in Thomas Storer's *The Life and Death of Thomas Wolsey Cardinall* (1599), for

Storer makes physical divisions in his metrical tragedy and names them "Wolseius aspirans," "Wolseius triumphans," and "Wolseius moriens."

In Shakespeare's tragedies this structure is especially evident in *Macbeth*, the peak of the pyramid being achieved with Macbeth's attaining the crown. In *Julius Caesar* the fortunes of Brutus and the conspirators rise to the assassination of Caesar; the fortunes of Coriolanus come to their highest point when Coriolanus is named consul; those of Romeo and Juliet mount to their marriage, while those of Antony are most favorable, not when he is closest to Cleopatra, but when he has married Octavia.

In *Titus Andronicus* the pyramidal movement is plainly embodied in the rising success of Tamora and her confederates; in this respect *Titus Andronicus* follows the plan of *The Spanish Tragedy*, for in both plays the revenge action serves to bring about the downfall of those who have climbed to high degree. *King Lear* is of similar construction: the pyramid is to be traced out in the fortunes of Goneril, Regan, and Edmund, even though the aspirers have become not nearly so interesting as their victims.

This suggests that along with the original pyramidal structure there was developed a concomitant or complementary structure which took the shape of an inverted pyramid; the revengers like Titus, a simple figure in a simple play, pursue such a downward and upward course. But Lear, a simple man in a complicated rôle, though his downward course is clear enough, can be said only in a peculiar fashion to pursue an upward course. Nevertheless he does, I think. With the scenes on the heath the audience must sense that at last Lear has slipped to the depths of misfortune, and in place of the restless, unreconciled feelings of pity and fear which it has had for him, it must now recognize the seal of fate upon him, must view him with compassion, with the firm and resolved understanding which is the end of tragedy. It will expect Lear, moreover, to give a sign that he sees himself in this same light, and its expectations are gratified; so it is that in terms of tragic realization Lear lifts himself from the depths.

This is to say that the pyramidal structure or its obverse is often to be detected in the audience's sense of the action rather than in the explicit events. Thus after the careful preparations in the first two acts of *Othello* the audience senses that the moment Othello attends to the first slanderous hint from the lips of Iago, he has begun his downward course. In achieving such composition *Othello* begins to resemble Greek tragedy, however much it differs from it in innumerable other ways; the audience, for instance, just as it responds to the first fatal motion of Othello, recognizes immediately that Agamemnon in treading the purple cloth laid upon his threshold has crossed into his doom. But Shakespeare usually follows the linear form of the metrical tragedy, balancing concrete action as the hero ascends the pyramid against concrete action as he descends; and *Hamlet*, beginning at a point equivalent to the first scene of the fourth act of *Titus Andronicus*, combines explicit deeds with the implicit psychological pyramid of *Othello*.

2. *An Extensive Action.* It is needless to say that Elizabethan tragedy employs an extensive action, and practically gratuitous, in view of the preceding paragraphs, to insist that the stimulus for such action originates in the metrical tragedies. But the inherent contrast of the ancient drama, which apparently grew out of choral recitals, and its intensive treatment of its materials, with the modern drama, which stemmed from a narrative art, and its consequent extensive treatment—this is worth the remark. This intrinsic nature of modern tragedy is what makes the formal five acts, the choruses, the unities, the stage decencies, and the other classical features effectively unassimilable; while on the other hand, since the Elizabethans felt tragedy to be an extended, rising and falling action, plots originating in works like the metrical romance and the *novella* were easily assimilable.

3. *A Dramatic Exposition.* Devoted to extensive treatment, Elizabethans endeavored to combine preliminary exposition—that is to say, the identification of time and place and characters and basic situation—with the framework of the main action. Every composition requires of course an introduction of some sort; the Senecan drama uses a frankly prologuizing first act, while the metrical tragedy begins with an abstract,

moralizing exposition. The English dramatists, convinced that everything could be converted into grist for their mills, begin directly with action. The procedure is hazardous, for nothing is more unsatisfactory than a scene in which the primary intent to convey information is ill disguised. But the Elizabethans, and especially Shakespeare, were skillful, and it is often difficult to tell where the exposition leaves off and the enacting of the real conflict begins, though it is usually towards the end of the first act.

The beginning of *Romeo and Juliet* provides a good example of the dramatic exposition. The basic situation, the enmity of the Montagues and Capulets, is acted out first of all in the street fighting; then Romeo displays his susceptibility to love; the Capulets go over their plans for Juliet's marriage; and finally the paths of the young Montague and the young Capulet come together. The brilliance of the technical accomplishment here is apparent; it is matched and perhaps surpassed in the later plays, and is possibly anticipated in *Titus Andronicus;* for the Roman play begins with a clash in the street of the basic factions in the situation, and immediately, though the real conflict rises much later, Titus assumes his essential rôle, that (if rather too elevated terms may be allowed) of magisterial authority caught between irreconcilable duties. The directness and vitality of this exposition, particularly in comparison with the faltering preliminaries in *The Spanish Tragedy*, suggest only the craftsmanship of Shakespeare.

Part of the liveliness of Shakespearean drama seems to result from a certain Gothic quality which makes its appearance in the expositions. Sometimes it is as if Shakespeare deliberately points us in the wrong direction, puts us off guard, and then overwhelms us with his true concerns or else makes us realize suddenly the real significance of things we have seen superficially. *Henry IV*, a drama of war, has for introduction a splendidly lyrical speech about peace; *King Lear* begins with easy ribaldry and extravagant magnanimity; news from Rome grates Antony but Cleopatra (ironically, of course, but not with simple irony) urges him to hear the messengers; Romeo is well nigh dead with love for a woman who is not Juliet; Macbeth, though he is to be undermined with fear, is a paragon of bravery; Othello's trouble seems to be Brabantio; Denmark's trouble seems to be the warlike threats of Fortinbras. This is effective strategy. It rests doubtless on the medieval apprehension of the sovereignty of change and the quirkiness of fortune. The metrical tragedies regularly begin with an exposition of the calmness and goodness which are shattered by the tragical movement, and more than that, those tragedies relating to the rise and fall of a king's concubine begin with an elaborate account of the woman's native chastity—an attack which is the opposite of the ancient treatment of the Phaedra story.

This exciting ambiguity as to the direction to be taken by the plot recurs within the body of the action, sometimes, where it should be least expected, just before the catastrophe. For though we know that catastrophe is inevitable, yet we are led at next to the last moment to hope that it may not be too late to save Cordelia and Lear himself, to hope faintly but with some reason that Antony's victory on land will have favorable consequences, that Hamlet's reconciliation with Laertes will reprieve him, and even to hope and fear that Macbeth will escape in his magic invulnerability.

On a larger and final scale these mixings of directions seem to be the principle underlying the phenomenon called "tragic relief." For the interruption of terrifying, intense events with low pitched or comic scenes produces, I think, a mixed effect which serves to enlarge the nervous excitement of the whole drama rather than to relieve the tension; to make the tragic structure vastly inclusive and perhaps therefore more easy to bear, rather than to hold it to severe periodic doses. Whether the phenomenon should be called tragic relief or not, it is obviously a Gothic principle, adapted from the older drama, from mystery and interlude, into the formal pattern of the medieval tragedy.[1]

4. *The Pyramidal Motive.* A peculiarity of the extensive construction is that it generates the dominant motive within itself, pushes it to an apex, and dissolves it in the death of the protagonist. The revenge tragedy furnishes the best illustrations. In *The Spanish Tragedy* the revenge motive is generated only after (a) Hieronimo has been wronged, (b) he has discovered the

identity of the murderers, and (c) he has exhausted the possibility of recourse to legal justice; then his vengeful plans take shape and work themselves out in the catastrophe. *Titus Andronicus* repeats this arrangement, with the difference that the original wrong done Titus is elaborately motivated. In *Hamlet* the narrative of the Ghost accounts for the generation of the motive; such condensing of the plot is rather plainly a late refinement, doubtless suggested, through an intermediate *Ur-Hamlet* stage, by such impressive treatment in *The Spanish Tragedy* as this:

> And art thou come, Horatio, from the deapth,
> To aske for iustice in this vpper earth. . . .? [2]

And we may be sure that any *Ur-Hamlet* enacted the murder of the old King Hamlet either at the end of the first act or in the course of the second.

This practice of rooting the motive in the action itself is a mark of the difference between the modern tragedy and the ancient: there is in later tragedy never anything like the rooting of the vengeful career of an Atreus or an Orestes in a curse laid upon a distant ancestor, or the misfortunes of a Phaedra or a Hercules in the doings of the gods. On the other hand the modern treatment makes tragedy a direct outgrowth of the disposition of the protagonist and the peculiar situation in which he finds himself; it reckons only with coherences of cause and effect, even though these coherences may seem to be overlaid by an ultimate fatality. It leads therefore to psychological drama in which the individual is obliged to accept practical responsibility for his deeds.

5. *The One-Man Play.* The medieval tragedy, being an account of a man's fall from high degree, developed into a drama with unparalleled stress upon a single personage. Probably the peculiar rhetoric achieved by blank verse—the oratory of pride, the rant inherited from the mysteries, the frenzied metaphors of Hieronimo—served to make decisive the separation of the leading character from the lesser personages, for obviously a Tamburlaine or a Macbeth speaks on a pitch which can be reached consistently by no one else. Thus the nature of the poetic medium is what would seem to make an essential difference between Elizabethan and French tragedy, which also rests, much more closely than is usually recognized, on medieval conceptions of tragedy. Shakespeare modifies long-standing conventions only to make room for the pairs of lovers. And this not especially significant departure, inaugurated by *Romeo and Juliet,* was prepared for, among other instances, by Chaucer's "little tragedy," *Troilus and Criseyde*, and Arthur Brooke's "tragical matter," the *Romeus and Juliet;* by metrical tragedies like Churchyard's *Jane Shore* and Daniel's *Rosamond;* by Marlowe's and Shakespeare's own tragical erotic poems—by these pieces, whatever may have been the contribution of an earlier play.[3] Since Elizabethans had the habit of lumping writers of history and tragedy together, the practice in the chronicle histories is of

secondary importance, though it certainly brought about technical enrichments; and it is interesting to observe that Shakespeare's histories are tragedies in effect when they approach or become, like *Richard III*, one-man plays.[4]

6. *The Single Dominating Passion.* In England the metrical tragedy resolved itself formally into a ghost's recital of his downfall; the arrangement is of course as old as Boccaccio's first contributions to *De Casibus* literature but it became the rule in Cavendish's *Metrical Visions* and in *The Mirror* and its numerous progeny. Such recitals inevitably took on a retrospective, peculiarly analytical character: no ghost, whether or not he made outcry against the unreasonableness of Fortune, could refrain from seeking out and laying particular stress upon some prepossessing quality in himself, some undermining fault, some dominant passion which led to his disaster; or if he was not specific enough, the recorders of his tale would make good the deficiency. The tendency is old: it is well illustrated in Gower's *Confessio Amantis*, and in the metrical tragedy it went to such extremes that Anthony Munday, in his pretentious *Mirrour of Mutabilitie, or Principall part of the Mirrour for Magistrates* (1579), fits a tragedy to each of the Seven Deadly Sins—King Nebuchadnezzar's dominating passion is pride; King Herod's, envy; King Pharaoh's, wrath; King David's, lechery . . .

This habit of looking at tragedy analytically, as an

ex post facto sequence of events, was a conditioning force which made Elizabethan tragedy different from any other. In almost all of Shakespeare's heroes "we observe a marked one-sidedness," Bradley writes, "a predisposition in some particular direction; a total incapacity, in certain circumstances, of resisting the force which draws in this direction; a fatal tendency to identify the whole being with one interest, object, passion, or habit of mind." And Bradley adds, "This, it would seem, is, for Shakespeare, the fundamental tragic trait."[5]

7. *Introspection.* A narrative of one's own fall from greatness would be strange if it were not introspective, and indeed the ghosts of the metrical tragedies possessed unlimited capacities for self-examination. The Ghost of Buckingham, for instance, makes as nice an analysis of the dominant and destructive passion which impelled him and Richard III in tragical events as we are likely to be able to make if we work from Shakespeare's tragedy on the same subject:

> Yet wee, that were so drowned in the depth
> Of deepe desire, to drinke the guiltelesse bloud,
> Like to the wolfe, with greedy lookes that lepth
> Into the snare, to feede on deadly foode . . .
> That blinde, wee sawe not our destruction playne.
> (Sackville's *Buckingham*, St. 25)

Such analysis, it should be observed, and explicit statement of theme—"And see if bloud ey aske not bloud agayne" (stanza 12)—had been accomplished forty years before Shakespeare wrote *Macbeth*.

Narrative introspective methods, however, were not easily adapted to the stage, and effective rendering of subjective data had to wait, I believe, until Kyd made the advance at which we have looked. Then, though *Titus Andronicus* was a relative failure, the way was opened for the reflective soliloquies of Hamlet and the bloody scruples of Macbeth; but meanwhile and always the blunt revelations of the narratives had their place in, for instance, the self-analysis of Richard III and the "motive-hunting" soliloquies, as Coleridge called them, of Iago.

Still, it is just as well that the dramatists were forced to a preponderantly objective treatment, that is, to objective and dramatic renderings of the inner matters which were of final interest to them; for, as it is, Elizabethan tragedy occupies a favorable position between the clear, cool objectivity of the ancients (Euripides partly excepted) and the turgid subjectivity of Seneca.

8. *The Evolving Character.* An extensive action, in contrast with the intensive action of the classical drama, allowed at least the *time* in which a character could develop or change. But an epic is also an extensive action; and, as Freytag has observed, a mark of the difference between epic or semi-epic and modern dramatic treatment is that the former lets its characters stand side by side while the latter causes them to influence and to change one another. Thus *Tamburlaine*,

say, and the first third of *The Spanish Tragedy* are epic.

And thus the metrical tragedy is by birthright dramatic. For, whether a Churchyard is telling of a woman's change from simplicity to adulterous regality, from this to vengeful remorsefulness, or whether a Sackville is recounting a man's—Buckingham's—deflection into lust for blood, his subsequent qualms, and his attempt at virtuous rebellion—these changes are tabulated first of all as the result of the influence of one person or another. So Othello is changed by Iago, Macbeth by Lady Macbeth, Brutus and Hamlet by the encircling pressures of many people. But it must be added promptly that Elizabethans conceived of change in character as something which could happen for no tabulatable reasons. This is an inherited view, common in the metrical tragedies, and, though we in our later judgment look at it askance, we must accept it if we are to make sense of such various characters as Cressida, Prince Hal, and Angelo; and if we are to understand how Othello could give credence to so black a change in Desdemona, Leontes in Hermione, and Claudio in Hero.

The changing character, or the evolving character in the sense of change towards increased complexity, affords still other grounds for distinction between the ancient and modern tragedy. Structurally the Greeks, beginning the drama after the modern climax, after the apex of the extensive, pyramidal form, and concentrating only on the kernel of the modern catastrophe, utilized an unfolding situation rather than change of any kind. Rather than a climax they employed what Aristotle calls a Reversal of the Situation: "thus in the Oedipus, the messenger comes to cheer Oedipus and free him from his alarms about his mother, but by revealing who he is, he produces the opposite effect." [6]

The difference, however, goes deeper. For the Greeks, as Freytag has said, the greatness of tragic heroes consisted, before all, in firmness; [7] the vacillation of Hamlet, the disintegration of Macbeth, the naked credulity of Othello would have repulsed Sophocles. And this indicates the final grounds for distinction: the Greeks (with the usual modifications in regard to Euripides), interested, as it is said, "in justifying the ways of God to man," had their eyes on the entangled tragic situation; and to clarify it, to grasp it as the terrific consequences of old sins as in Aeschylus or as the divine readjustment of man's presumptions as in Sophocles—this was their end, not the revelation of what the individual man himself is. Naturally if they were to cleave such essentially religious problems they needed a firm protagonist, one whose personal character would not distract attention from the larger matters. Elizabethan—and modern—interests are otherwise of course. Hamlet, at a peak of tragic bewilderment, exclaims, "What a piece of work is a man!" and has nothing serious to say about the ways of God. But this also seems to be true: though men in Shakespeare's tragedies are peculiar, changeable, infirm, one-sided, subject alike to sweeping normal influences and to the most special pressures, still they are more than individuals; they have a certain universality, and consequently, since what happens to them happens more or less to all men, they do perform the equivalent of revealing, and justifying, the ways of God.

This is not to say that the Greek dramatists practiced an abstract art; the concreteness of their work can be determined best by thinking of it beside the Senecan plays and the metrical tragedies, both of which exist only too often for the sake of moralizations expressed in elaborate and merely verbal formulas. But the ancients aimed ultimately at explicit speculation, while Shakespeare is definitely puzzling when he is explicitly speculative, or rather appears to be so, as in Hamlet's "To be or not to be . . ." or in the reechoing thought, "As flies to wanton boys, are we to the gods," in *King Lear* (IV, 1, 36), and is comparatively lucid by implication. The ancients also ground their characters on the typical and make them become concrete by fitting them to direct action, while Shakespeare grounds his characters on the individual and makes them become typical by building up expressive correlatives for their interior and universal natures; though, again, they are only implicitly typical. The procedures are reversed, the final differences not very great.

9. *The Wholly Wicked Character.* At first glance Shakespeare's characters of unadulterated evil, like

Aaron, Iago, and Iachimo, seem to be the progeny of the Vices in the moral plays, and when one, making allowances at the same time for Shakespeare's inspired treatment, considers their sheer delight in evil and the propulsive parts which they play, their ancestry stands in no great doubt. But, thus seen, the connection is probably too direct and too simple. There is always Richard III to remind us that the totally wicked character is no mere adaptation of a conventional figure in the older drama; for behind him lie, it is equally apparent, such ruthless "tyrants" as King Cambyses and the Richard of Sackville's *Buckingham.*[8] Consequently we must suppose that Shakespeare's complete villains are molded most importantly by the enduring medieval view that the evil of the world could and did manifest itself in wholly evil human beings.

Glaring villainy on the part of a primary personage is a peculiar phenomenon in great drama, and, as Lessing originally observed, remarkably contradictory to the principles of Aristotle. To use villainy, moreover, as the single mainspring of tragic action is even more exceptional, for it would seem to lead to crude, superficial, black and white, unmotivated melodrama. In *Othello* for instance, whether we leap with Coleridge to the conclusion that Iago represents motiveless malignity or whether we try to inject a little psychological reality into him by remarking on his "good" qualities, like his courage and intelligence, the result is nearly the same—Iago is evil without qualification or he is evil enlivened by a fearful perversion of good abilities; in all common sense we should say that one way lies plain melodrama, while the other way lies melodrama founded on a psychological monstrosity. But *Othello* is neither of these things. *Othello* is serious, universal, and flawlessly motivated. There is only one explanation of this: the wholly wicked character was for Shakespeare a serious reality, and Iago, unlike the creations of melodrama, was essential to a serious view, the medieval view of the world. We accept Iago because the world is re-created for us from that point of view.

It is, of course, a world of unusual vitality. Vitality, in fact, has so crept into the conception of Iago that he is a character of mixed qualities, though the mixing makes no final difference. This indicates, I think, that the medieval apprehension or sense of total evil (but probably not the idea of evil) was in a process of change. Hence the extraordinary disposition of Claudius in *Hamlet:* Claudius, according to the Ghost and according to Hamlet himself, is a creature of ultimate blackness, darker, it would seem, than Richard or Iago. But we would say otherwise because of the vivid sensory apprehension of Claudius that Shakespeare has given us. Here, then, is a split between idea and sense, the former remaining "medieval," the latter becoming "modern"; a split, but not a contradiction, which seems to reside in the heart of the Shakespearean genius. It creates a part of the limitless complexity of *Hamlet*, for we see Claudius through the eyes of Hamlet, we share in *the idea* of Claudius, and at the same time we are stirred by our feelings about him as a man. So also with Shylock. This split was probably an underground rumbling; probably no one was conscious of it, not even Shakespeare: to the conscious mind Claudius was a villain, an incarnation of evil.

10. *The Catastrophe.* A definitive condition in modern tragedy is that it ends with death. The ancient drama, occupied with a tragic situation rather than one man's journey up and down the grim pyramid, could achieve its effect with or without death; indeed *Oedipus Tyrannus* is more tragic in the way that *Hamlet* or *King Lear* is tragic than is *Oedipus Coloneus*, though Oedipus lives through the former drama and dies in the latter. But the bequest of the metrical tragedy was not simply a final death scene; as a rule it was instead a general loosening of the forces of death, a repercussive slaughter led up to by earlier bloodshed. The culmination in boundless horror was deliberately sought out: the account of Pompey in the Boccaccio-Lydgate literature is a masterpiece of the gruesome, ranging from the description of the ghost with his face disfigured and soiled by smoke and sea-water to the account of the display of the impaled head in Alexandria. And a huge slaughter was accepted casually by Chaucer's Monk as the perfectly natural end of the tragedy of Samson:

> This is to seyn, the prynces everichoon,
> And eek thre thousand bodyes, were ther slayn
> With fallynge of the grete temple of stoon.

This had to be so because tragedy was meant to illustrate the essential horror of life and the reasons for a Contempt of the World morality. In its essential aspects medieval tragedy was—to borrow the figure from Professor Farnham's brilliant exposition of this point—a Dance of Death.

With this fundamental tradition as to the nature of the tragic, it follows that any story of lavish violence could provide the crude stuff of drama, and that the violence enacted on the Elizabethan stage springs first of all from the adaptation of narrative stuffs to the needs of actors. Precedent for, and practice in, direct adaptation were supplied by the mysteries, moralities, and interludes. Or in terms of principles the situation may be described thus: The conception of the nature and form of tragedy was inherited from nondramatic literature, while some incidental technique was borrowed from the older drama. To these principles, the contribution of Seneca, which I think was insignificant, must in any event have been secondary, as also the probably more important contribution of the contemporary French and Italian tragedy, itself subject in its classicism to modification by these same principles. It is, for example, primarily the medieval conception of what was tragic that motivates the slaughter at the end of *The Spanish Tragedy* and, for that matter, *Titus Andronicus* and *Hamlet*. This, I think, is true, even though the meaning of the slaughter may have been seen only dimly, or, more likely, even though the medieval significance, which would have men contemn the world and turn to other-worldliness, was revised in ways which will be discussed shortly.

One characteristic mark of the medieval tragedy reappears with astonishing conspicuousness in several of the Shakespearean catastrophes. It is the plea of the protagonist that his story be told to the world; the familiar words of Hamlet are a good example:

> Horatio, I am dead;
> Thou liv'st; report me and my cause aright
> To the unsatisfied . . .
> Absent thee from felicity awhile,
> And in this harsh world draw thy breath in pain,
> To tell my story.

So also Othello, with the addition of spectacular self-analysis. Now the complaining ghosts of the metrical tragedy regularly make this same plea for widespread attention to their stories. "Sackville," says the Ghost of Buckingham, "mark well my fall, and paint it forth that all estates may know . . ." The ghosts are interested, of course, in having their causes reported aright because of the morality which they illustrate. The Ghost of Rosamond tells Daniel to write

> the ruine of my youth,
> Report the downe-fall of my slippry state:
> Of all my life reueale the simple truth,
> To teach to others, what I learnt too late:
> Exemplifie my frailtie, tell howe Fate
> Keepes in eternall darke our fortunes hidden,
> And ere they come, to know them tis forbidden.[9]

They are interested, too, in seeing justice done their reputations in the world; Rosamond, for instance, complains that she has not been so fortunate as Shore's wife, whose tragedy, as told by Churchyard in *The Mirror*, Rosamond says, "justifies her foul attaint."

These requests of the ghosts look, then, in two directions: towards the didactic import of their falls and towards the establishment of a correct, analytical understanding of their fatal weaknesses. It is the same with Shakespeare, except that his handling of these perorations is so lifelike, so suited to the particular character, that the didacticism is absent or not conspicuous. The dying Hotspur, whose words like Hamlet's are cut off by the fell sergeant, still is able to manage a perfect and dramatic synopsis of his own faulty character:

> I better brook the loss of brittle life
> Than those proud titles thou hast won of me,

and Prince Hal furnishes the moral, the substance of which, but not the language, had been the final word in many a metrical tragedy:

> Ill-weaved ambition, how much art thou shrunk.

Othello's concern about what report of him will be made merges strikingly into an analytical statement of his failings:

> When you shall these unlucky deeds relate,
> Speak of me as I am; nothing extenuate,
> Nor set down aught in malice: then, must you speak

Of one that lov'd not wisely but too well;
Of one not easily jealous, but, being wrought,
Perplex'd in the extreme . . .

(V, 2, 340–5)

Thus it would seem that the Shakespearean catastrophe borrows on occasion the conventional formula, "Tell my story," from the metrical tragedy, but that the formula is of far less importance than, and is contingent upon, the backwards summarizing glance which the fallen protagonist casts upon his own character and actions. And this itself is but another manifestation of the Elizabethan and medieval way of seeing tragedy, that is, retrospectively, analytically, as an *ex post facto* series of events—the way, in fact, which contributes the one-sidedness to the heroic characters.

T. S. Eliot puts a good deal of stress on these analytical departing speeches. For him they are dyed deep with the spirit, if not with the direct influence, of Seneca. "Antony says," Eliot writes, " 'I am Antony still,' and the Duchess, 'I am Duchess of Malfy still'; would either of them have said that unless Medea had said *Medea superest?*" [10] This is one of the pivots on which Eliot's Shakespearean criticism turns; he uses the findings of Senecan scholarship and lets them appear to be much more certain than they ever were; thus he is able to characterize the Elizabethan age as "a period of dissolution and chaos," [11] and then to make this assertion, "If Shakespeare had written according to a better philosophy, he would have written worse poetry; it was his business to express the greatest emotional intensity of his time, based on whatever his time happened to think." [12] We cannot deny that the pre-Shakespearean period suffered its share of dissolution, and we can understand that, for Eliot, this may always be the predominant fact about it; but we can also see, I think, that while it was declining in certain respects it was recovering in other ways. We can say at least that Eliot's position, in so far as it depends on Senecan research, is badly grounded: we have no very definite reasons as yet to be so sure that Elizabethan philosophy as a whole was bad or that it was much influenced by bad philosophy. And we can and should look further into Eliot's pivotal assumption, that the self-awareness in the final speeches of Shakespeare's heroes is an attitude of stoic pride.

Certainly unusual self-awareness is an elemental condition in Elizabethan tragic heroes. But it seems to be a final, retrospective self-awareness, a drawing together of things, and an expository achievement handed down from the narrative tragedy; and it seems not to be a manifestation of pride, of extravagant and romantic individualism. For the self-identification is a means to the definitely ethical end of saying, "Thus and thus I was, thus and thus I met my fall." The process is illustrated most fully by one of the earliest of Shakespeare's catastrophes, by Richard III's retrospections after his ominous medieval-symbolic dream:

> Fool, of thyself speak well: fool, do not flatter.
> My conscience hath a thousand several tongues,
> And every tongue brings in a several tale,

And every tale condemns me for a villain.
Perjury, perjury, in the high'st degree:
Murder, stern murder, in the dir'st degree;
All several sins, all us'd in each degree,
Throng to the bar, crying all, 'Guilty! Guilty!'
(V, 3, 193–200)

Moreover, the self-analysis and the self-identification are condensed into a single line:

Richard loves Richard; that is, I am I.
(V, 3, 184)

This position can be supported by an examination of non-Shakespearean treatment. Unusual self-consciousness marks the hero's conduct in the catastrophes of serious tragedy; Kyd's Hieronimo and Marlowe's Edward seem to illustrate the rule. The exception is Marlowe's Faustus. And the inference to be drawn is that Faustus is an exceptional hero in an exceptional drama, a drama that uses such conspicuously medieval materials as the Seven Deadly Sins and the other visions and at the same time is decidedly unconventional in spirit. In the catastrophe Marlowe overstepped the bounds of accepted form just as he upset convention by allowing the proud Tamburlaine to escape a catastrophic fall: Faustus' death is presented in fairly immediate, naturalistic, and romantic terms, while the deaths of the other heroes are in regular and formal terms.

In comparing the catastrophe, as the other structural features, of Elizabethan tragedy with the *De Casibus* literature, we must distinguish between formula and living convention, between formality and form. I think that the Elizabethans wrote the sort of tragedy they wrote because of a general absorption in the form and limitations of the *De Casibus* story: they wrote tragedy as they saw and felt tragedy. The narratives of falls were, as it has been said, Dances of Death; similarly, and for almost the same reasons, the typical tragedy at the end of the sixteenth century was a Tragedy of Blood.

CHAPTER V

SOME PRINCIPLES OF ETHICAL FORM IN PRE-SHAKESPEAREAN TRAGIC LITERATURE

THE SENECANISM ingrained in so many chapters of criticism is scarcely the product of specific structural data; it is rather, I think, a generalization which sprang up in spite of evidence and which rested on the false principle that stage plays are an exclusive category in themselves. It is a general feeling, and a general feeling, it might be remarked, which was wholly congenial to the romantic critics, the followers of Augustus Schlegel, who were intent upon setting Shakespeare off from classical, and indeed from all, predecessors; and congenial also to the newer scientific critics who, being still very awkward at their work, had to practice with the most mechanical and unimportant details.

So much for the negative side of critical Senecanism. On the positive side "Senecan" must be recognized as an epithet used to describe the effect of the imperfect English tragedy at *c.* 1590. Here, whether or not the epithet is accurate, it has some attractions, for the late sixteenth century developed a popular tragedy which in spirit resembles the Senecan plays. But it is also fundamentally different. Clarity in this distinction entails the study of evasive matters and the consideration of very long processes: distinction between the *effects* of a play by Kyd and of a comparable one by Seneca lies, I take it, in the field of esthetic and moral significance, and is, consequently, overshrouded with difficulty. Yet even a tentative sketch may have a value in itself and may open the way to improved understanding of Shakespearean tragedy.

I.

In spite of the need of simplicity and directness here, it is difficult to treat Seneca's stoicism except as an unreclaimable bog of paradoxes. It contains one principle, however, which gives us an opening for a certain simplification. Examine for instance its fundamental proposition: that the world is a structure of goodness, with the divine immanent in it; yet the lives of people show that for them the events of the world are bad. This paradox, it will be noticed, has a theoretic or ideal side and a contradictory practical side, and this, I think, is the key to Seneca's thought. But the practical will always overwhelm the theoretical where there is rivalry between them: it did so for Seneca himself, and in the medieval attention to Seneca it seems to have obliterated the theoretical; consequently it is most important to us.

In practical terms, then, the world is evil. Men act under the lash of irrational Fortune; they may know in some remote, glimmering corner of their minds that Fortune is in reality Divine Providence, but its ways are so dark that the bare thought of scrutinizing it at work would be naïve folly. Men are lashed on to commit the bloodiest of deeds; over these they have no control—though they have freedom of the will. For their freedom is mostly a moral freedom, a freedom, that is to say, to endure the whims of a disastrous world with resignation; otherwise they have one praiseworthy act within their powers—suicide. The stoic, finding in himself this combination of limitations and powers, retreats into a moral attitude, into the familiar attitude of stoic pride, which rests on the determination to believe oneself unmaterial, sharing in the divine spirit, a thing totally apart from the world. Beside this, an indeed devious sort of pride, it should be noted that the pride of Tamburlaine rests on a positive relationship to the world, and similarly that the self-conscious speeches of Shakespeare's dying heroes are statements of tragic relationships to other human beings.

It is in the sphere of practical worldly conduct, nevertheless, that stoicism flourishes. Be passive, be lowly, be in connection with the world untouched and untouching; thus you may manifest your handful of divinity, thus, in a proud apartness. As tinged with degeneracy as this attitude is, the next step in the scheme—the step which we are obliged to think was most important to Seneca—is actively perverse. Be passive, be lowly—and thus you will attain worldly power; be humble and rule others. When, in a characteristic passage which was forced on our attention earlier, Agamemnon urges Pyrrhus not to sacrifice

Polyxena,[1] what is Agamemnon's argument? In the version of Jasper Heywood it is this:

> The proude estate of tyranny
>   may never long endure.
> The King that rules with modest meane
>   of safety may be sure.
>
> (*N.'s S.*, II, 22)

In other words the stoic conceals himself from Fortune by keeping his head bent very low. He works towards prosperity by scorning prosperity. If he enjoys high place, he counts it so much won; if he slips from high place, he changes his system of accounting and writes down no loss.

This is a slippery philosophy, full of pride and timidity, of desperate craft and pitiful self-delusion. Viewed in the most favorable light, it equips one always to be prepared for the worst; like the boxer's technique of riding back and away from blows, it is valuable on occasion but is only a defensive device. It has its sad place in the world when men are kept on the defensive, either because of the onslaughts of a chaotic society, like Seneca's, or because of personal difficulties. One may be sympathetic with Seneca and yet say, as one must say, that his is Greek philosophy reborn and deformed. It is what the Golden Mean came to, what Sophocles' struggle against presumption and what Aeschylus' vision of eternal justice came to.

The morbidity of the Senecan plays follows inevitably from this intellectual and moral system. Only think how it would be to look on the world as totally evil in its physical manifestations and yet at the same time, in some secret fashion, as essentially good; it is an unholy contradiction, in effect something like looking on a corpse. Or think how it would be to retreat, intent upon a self-assumed strain of divinity, into the corner of apartness and from there to view the harsh events of the world; all that is unpleasant would be seen grotesquely magnified, horrible, unreasonable, and hopeless; for the pleasure to be taken in an escape is equal to one's measurement of the dangers retreated from. Therefore, if you are a Seneca you will say, let the blood flow, let the furies prevail, for all this is what I am different from; the worse these things, the better off am I. Hence the fascination with evil. We in this age should find no difficulty in understanding Seneca's psychological and spiritual morbidity; for not only do we have in the Sunday supplements the lurid pages which pretend to be exposures of vice, but we also have serious novels which exploit the glamor of evils in society while ostensibly attacking them, and poetry which hopes to correct disorder by imitating it; and we have too those world philosophies which answer present difficulties by calling for, on the one hand, a retreat into the apartness of the racial past and, on the other hand, a promotion of the violences and hatreds of the present—attitudes which seek a mystical identity of the individual with a race and which deify that race by bedeviling other races. Morbid stoicism is the refuge of the defeated; its doctrine is, the worse the world, the better I.

2.

Or, in the usual phrase, stoicism is the philosophy of slaves. As such—to make no bones about a delicate matter—it probably made its large contributions to early Christianity. I shall not dwell on the similarities except to say what is perfectly obvious, that the early Christians were an oppressed people who had a great need for a scheme of things in which they could stand apart, resigned, inconspicuously guarding their inner light; whether Biblical meekness was ever equivalent to the Senecan crafty humility, or similar, for instance, to the Sophoclean religious virtue, I do not know, though I imagine that it was as various as the temperaments which espoused it.

But the differences between Christianity and stoicism are important and, by the time which is relevant to our study, the time, say, of Boccaccio, they are not confusing. The world is wholly evil, with no paradoxes about a pantheistic goodness in it. It is subject to change, to change rather than to the malevolent reversals of the Senecan self-dramatizing view, though no less disastrous to the aspirations of man. Change is worked chiefly, according to the level from which it is viewed, by Fortune, by the stars, and ultimately by Divine Providence; it is inscrutable, not because it is malevolence, but because its processes are beyond the ken of man, and it is, after all, only one of the most striking reminders of sinful man's unhappy condition in a sinful world. Yet a particularly wicked man may call down a direct punishment upon himself, and upon his innocent associates as well.

The essential differences come to this: The human being in his humanness partakes of the evil of the world. Therefore in calling the world evil he calls himself evil; his attitude is one of genuine humility, not a disguise for pride; for pride, of course, is the first of deadly sins. Then, and all the other principles rest on this one, in exalting death as a liberation from the Devil, the Flesh, and the World, the Christian is exalting the hope of life after death, the hope of immortality with its manifold promises. Whether or not all this is benumbing to human action, good as well as bad, it is certainly not a morbid self-contradiction. There is at least straight thinking in the formulation, the worse the world, the worse am I.

Though Christianity reversed the central ideas of the stoics, much of the incidental ethics is taken over bodily. The fickleness of fortune, the hazards of ambition, the terrors of high place, the rashness of youth—these and the kindred subjects favored by Seneca are accepted for their face-value, as evidence, that is, that the world is untrustworthy; they are accepted thus, so far as general truth goes, with pure simplicity, not with an eye to deluding Fortune while snatching up a few of the world's favors. This also seems to be the spirit in which these precepts are accepted in the greater part of sixteenth-century literature.

And the Senecan plays fell similarly into the large, loose category of medieval tragedy. They were only other, neither better nor worse, documents illustrating the plight of fallen humanity in general and the impressive leveling of the mighty in particular. The theoretic or ideal meaning of the plays, from the notion of immanent goodness in evil actualities to the satisfaction to be taken in prideful detachment—these things which became for Seneca himself dim verbal formulas in the glare of much sensationalism, now passed quite unnoticed. The shrewd maxims of conduct, where they were not immediately assimilable, offered no problem; for no one could suspect for a moment that Pyrrhus would be able to heed the canny (though not disinterested) advice of Agamemnon, that Thyestes would recognize the practical wisdom in his misgivings and refuse the crown, or that Jason would have the good sense to insure his prosperity by paying off his debt to Medea. Worldly wisdom, as each Senecan catastrophe proved, also fits into the pattern of *vanitas vanitatum.*

3.

I have been suggesting that Elizabethans looked on Seneca in much the same way that their ancestors looked on him. The introduction here of some contemporary commentary, or as nearly contemporary as possible, will clarify both the nature of stoicism and its place in Elizabethan schemes of values, that is to say, in those schemes of values which received a deliberate and conscious formulation. The dramatists were not philosophers, of course; and they have left very meager records of what they thought of stoicism. But, in the absence of evidence to the contrary, the only sane hypothesis is that in general they thought what their contemporaries were thinking. Of what this was, the documents bearing on Seneca's moral treatises are at least fully intelligible.

Henry Peacham approves highly of both Seneca and Plutarch. His reasons for admiring Seneca have been much undercut by modern scholarship, but in 1634 when Peacham wrote *The Compleat Gentleman*, his view was doubtless still the popular view:

For Morality and rules of well living, delivered with such sententious gravity, weight of reason, so sweetned with lively and apt similitudes, entertaine *Plutarch;* whom according to the opinion of *Gaza* the world would preserve, should it be put to the choice to receive one onely Author (the Sacred Scriptures excepted) and to burne all the rest: especially his *Lives* and *Morals*. After him, the vertuous and divine *Seneca*, who for that he lived so neere the times of the Apostles, and had familiar acquaintaince with S. *Paul* (as it is supposed by those Epistles that passe under either names) is thought in heart to have beene a Christian; and *certes* so it seemeth to me, by that Spirit, wherewith so many rules of Patience, Humility, Contempt of the world, are refined and exempt from the degrees of Paganisme. Some say that about the beginning of *Neroes* raigne, he came over hither into *Britaine:* but most certaine it is, he had divers lands bestowed on him here in *England*, and those supposed to have laine in Essex neere to *Camalodunum*, now *Maldon.*[2]

In making Seneca not only a Christian but an English landlord as well, Peacham has carried medieval traditions to the extreme. It is clear that for a man of his simplicity, actual stoicism does not exist as a philosophy: Seneca has been transformed into a saint who knows only the Christian virtues of Patience, Humility, and Contempt of the World. It is clear too that these virtues have become petrified formulas, for contempt of the world simply does not make sense in a treatise addressed to the complete gentleman.

Henry Peacham instructs us in the stereotypes of Elizabethan thought. On the other hand the active forms of the thought of the period are discernible, I think, in the Senecan translations of Thomas Lodge; and since Lodge was both a man of rich intellectual powers and a thorough artist in the fields we are considering, his opinions are doubly significant.

Lodge writes about Seneca, moreover, with warmth and genuine eloquence. He does not do lip service to the attitude of contempt of the world, but in his distress at the vanity of his world, he feels that Seneca, if he is read with discrimination, can contribute to the reformation of men. I quote somewhat at length from Lodge's preface to *The Workes of Lvcius Annaevs Seneca, Both Morrall and Naturall* (1614):

It was well donne by Nature (gentle Reader) to giue time, but ill donne by men not to apprehend the same: How much thou hast lost in life in begetting vanities and nourishing them, in applauding follies, and intending them, read heare; and begin now to apprehend this, that it is but lost life, that men liue in entertaining vaine things, & that no time is better spent, the*n* in studying how to liue, and how to die wel. This shalt thou learne in our *Seneca,* whose diuine sentences, wholsome counsailes, serious exclamations against vices, in being but a Heathen, may make vs ashamed being Christians; when wee consider how backward a course wee haue runne from the right scope, by being buried in vaine readings, besotted with selfe opinion, by apprehending vertue no more, but in a shadow, which serues for a vaile to couer many vices. It is lost labour in most men now-a-dayes whatsoeuer they haue studied, except their actions testifie that readings haue amended the ruines of their sicke and intemperate thoughts: and too pregnant a proofe is it, of an age and time ill spent, when as after a man hath summed vp the account of his dayes that are past, hee findeth the remainder of his profites, hee should haue gotten in life, to be eyther ambition vnsatisfied, or dissolution attended by pouerty, or vaine vnderstanding boulstered by pride, or irksome age called on by surfet; I must confesse that (had I effected it) I could haue pickt out eyther an author more curious, or a subiect more pleasing for common eares, to allure and content them. But seeing the worlds Lithargie so farre growne, that it is benummed wholly with false appearance, I made choice of this author, whose life was a pattern of continence, whose doctrine a detection and correction of vanities, and whose death a certaine instance of constancy. Would God Christians would endeuour to practise his good precepts, to reform their own in seeing his errours; and perceiuing so great light of learning from a Pagans pen, ayme at the true light of devotion and pietie, which becommeth Christians. Learne in him these good lessons, and commit them to memory, That to be truely vertuous is to be happy, to subdue passion is to be truely a man, to contemne fortune is to conquer her, to foresee and vnmaske miseries in their greatest terrors is to lessen them, to liue well is to be vertuous, and to die well is the way to eternitie. . . .[3]

However cautiously we frame our observations on this material, it is certain always that the elements of stoical morality are incidental to a different and a larger scheme of values—that is, according to Lodge's assertion, to Christianity. The assertion, however, if we apply it to the dramatists, raises more questions than it answers. Suppose that we were able to pin down the dramatists to a conscious formulation of their beliefs; they might very likely profess along with Lodge that they were governed finally by Christian theology and ethics, but even so we could not be certain that such profession would represent those inmost workings of the spirit which might appear in dramas but of which the authors themselves might not be consciously aware. And after all, "Christianity" is far too broad a term to be of any use to us in our consideration of the drama.

Lodge gives us, however, some important hints as to the solution of these difficulties. The specific evils which he condemns, for instance, are those common to medieval and Elizabethan literature—ambition, vain understanding and pride, dissolution and poverty, surfeit and premature old age. On these subjects Lodge finds Seneca eloquent and helpful. So might have been countless other authors, among them, as we have seen, Thomas Sackville. Here, indeed, seems to be another example of the traditional regard for the incidental ethics of stoicism.

In other ways Lodge seems to express lucidly a certain breaking away from medieval traditions. His moral indignation is directed, not in loose verbal terms at the world in general, but very specifically at his immediate world. Thus he is able to put especial emphasis on virtuous conduct; when he says, "To die well is the way to eternity,"[4] what *eternity* means to him is ambiguous, but his interest in a way of conducting oneself at the approach of death is not. Similarly, the ideal of being "truly a man" can be taken as a manifestation of the Renaissance. So, as a whole, he appears in the strong final sentence in the passage above, to be standing for an attitude of sober wisdom, of restraint, and of stern disapproval for his world. These virtues are readily comparable with stoic doctrine. They are also central, I think, to the ethical structures in the great Elizabethan tragedies.

The question is, then, where do Lodge and Seneca part ways? We must wonder whether a sentence like this one—"To contemn fortune is to conquer her"—means the same thing to Lodge that it would have meant to Seneca. The answer is to be found, I believe, in Lodge's translation, particularly in the brief appendix which lists what Elizabethans seem to have regarded as the chief points of difference between their thought and Senecan thought. The following selection from the appendix is relevant to our immediate purpose as well as to other pages in this study:

A Table Wherein Senecaes Paradoxes and other Stoicall vanities are set downe, to the end that such as are of weakest iudgement and apprehension, may both know. and be more circumspect in iudging of them.

10. That no man is good, wicked, or vngratefull.
11. All men are vngratefull.
16. Of fatal destinie.
18. Death is in the power and will of a man to kill himselfe, and to depart out of this world when hee thinketh fit, without expecting the good will and pleasure of God.
23. Mercie or compassion is an imperfection of the soule of affections.
28. That a wise-man ought not to intermeddle with affairs of estate.
30. Death is neither good nor euill, for that may bee either good or euill which is something, but that which is nothing, and reduceth all things to nothing, neyther subiecteth vs to good or to euill.
39. God dwelleth in euery good man, but we know not what God he is.
52. *Iupiter* can doe no more then a wise-man.
64. This world wherin we are contayned, is one, is God, whose members and companions we are.
65. A dead man is no more.

The Elizabethan rejection of some of these paradoxes seems to clinch certain points that we have already discussed. Rejection of the tenth—"that no man is good, wicked, or ungrateful"—agrees nicely with our treatment of characters like Aaron, Iago, and Iachimo. Disagreement with the twenty-third, on mercy or compassion, supports the position which we took in regard to the speeches on the theme, "Sweet mercy is nobility's true badge" (*T.A.*, I, 1, 119). To negate the fifty-second, comparing Jupiter with the wise man, indicates that the terms *God* and *the gods* are practically interchangeable. The treatment accorded still others has a general significance which we ought to take into account. Condemnation of the twenty-eighth, for instance, affirms the social and political responsibilities of the wise man. Opposition to the sixteenth, "of fatal destiny," shows that Elizabethans, at least in their conscious minds, were antideterministic.

Such direct denial of central principles in Seneca's philosophy may have been set down thus in a table chiefly for the sake of policy. One can easily see that Seneca's defense of suicide could scarcely have been let go unchallenged. But it would be a perverse subtlety to imagine that Lodge really approved of the paradoxes which stand thus explicitly rejected. And it is remarkable how directly and completely the maker of this table, and of the marginal notes to the text as well, cuts away the very heart of Senecan doctrine. At no place, neither in connection with the thirty-ninth paradox above, nor the sixty-fourth—"This world wherein we are contained, is one, is God, whose members and companions we are"—does the editor give an inch of credit to the notion of the exaltation of the individual human soul, to that notion from which the rest of Senecan stoicism proceeds.

This basic difference between Senecan and Elizabethan thought comes out very clearly indeed in the marginal comment on a passage in the *Consolation to*

Helvia. The passage itself is worth quoting as an illustration of Seneca's powers at their best (that he has his own large strain of eloquence we have doubtless not sufficiently acknowledged):

Belieue whosoeuer hath created this vniuers, whether it be that Almighty God, whether it be incorporall reason, that Workmaster of great things, whether it be a demy spirit, equally extended and spred amidst all great and small Creatures, whether it be Destiny, and this immutable succession of things enchained the one within the other: such a one hath caused that no things (except they be things most abiect and of little worth) are not out of our power. All that which is good in man, is not subiect to humane power and violence, which neither can giue it, or take it away. Nature hath created this world which is the greatest and fairest thing a man may see, But as touching the soule that contemplateth and admireth the world, whereof she is the most excellent part, she is proper vnto vs, shee is perpetuall and shall continue so long with vs, as we continue: let vs goe forward willingly and confidently, whethersoeuer our fortune leadeth vs; let vs march forward with a confident pace.[5]

Worldliness and unworldliness; man has nothing and everything within his power; his soul is of the world yet not of it: the marginal note goes sharply to the point in religious terms and, as it seems to me, in philosophical terms: "*A doubtfull opinion of* Seneca, *as touching the Deity, and his ordinary Paradox, tying the first cause which is God to secondary causes, reade here with aduice.*"

We may say with whatever confidence a coherent

contemporary document demands, that men in this period understood the root proposition of Senecanism and rejected it. To define the human soul as a dimensionless parcel of God was unacceptable; it follows that there were no grounds for developing an attitude of stoic pride. On the other hand subordinate aspects of stoicism were fully acceptable—when, it appears, they added to the many variations on old themes. Another marginal note in Lodge's *Seneca* says this: "Laugh at the absurdities, pitie his ignorance, embrace the best." [6]

4.

If we add here the few important contemporary references to the connection between the early English tragedies and the Senecan drama, we shall finally have come to the end of what appear to be the available materials bearing on the problem of the influence of Seneca.

Sir Philip Sidney's comparison of the style of *Gorboduc* with Seneca's style is not to be taken too seriously in view of the notorious Elizabethan weakness for showy comparisons. And any special eminence which might seem to be implied in the remark is denied in several ways. In his discussion of structural principles in the drama Sir Philip studies only Euripides, Plautus, and Terence—these authors, with no distinction between comedy and tragedy, which is in itself good support for our argument that the form of the English tragedy is derived in its most obvious aspects from the classical comedy. He also says that tragedy, "with sturring the affects of admiration and commiseration, teacheth, the vncertainety of this world, and vpon how weake foundations guilden roofes are builded" [7]—a description which, except for the Aristotelian note, echoes the Middle Ages and seems to deny the theoretic Renaissance seizing upon Seneca.

Thomas Nashe's bewildering and enticing famous page is another matter.[8] Aiming at malicious innuendo in its gibe at an author or authors who found that "English *Seneca* read by candle light yeeldes manie good sentences, as *Bloud is a begger*," it will probably always defy assured interpretation. But a few things are clear. If Seneca was held in the veneration that modern criticism proposes, it hardly stands to reason that Nashe would pick him for the club with which to beat his dependents; if the phrase "Bloud is a begger" is to be ridiculed, it is always Seneca's phrase. Again, Nashe insists on the English Seneca; it is not so with the modern scholars. Their criticism has thrived in the obscurity that separates the Latin from the English medium; those parallels with Newton's *Seneca* which have been proposed to date are first of all strikingly few and secondly because of peculiarities in style and the sharpness (sharpness, not accuracy) of the renderings, they usually confess their inadequacy aloud. Doubtless there is some truth in Nashe's charges; but it is difficult to say how those charges, be they exaggerations or not, relate to our present problem. They are apparently not grounds for maintaining that Seneca was the motivating influence behind Elizabethan tragedy, not even the Tragedy of Blood. They hint only that certain writers borrowed lines and speeches; Kyd appears to have been one of these writers. But borrowing goes almost without saying. It is profitable to reflect, when the problem of borrowing from Seneca comes up, that Marlowe, as J. M. Robertson pointed out, put five lines of the *Faerie Queene* (I, vii, 32) into *Tamburlaine* (4098–4103).

After all, we may as well take Nashe's word for it: Seneca contributed handfuls of tragical speeches. If the lost *Hamlet*, to which Nashe seems to be referring, is another play like for instance *The Misfortunes of Arthur*, Nashe, for all his wrath, is not even guilty of exaggeration. This is as far as we need go. We have very good reasons to believe that Seneca contributed rhetorical patches and practically nothing more; certainly nothing tangible to the form of the English tragedy; certainly nothing worth mentioning to its philosophy. Seneca, finally, like Machiavelli, seems to have been dragged by main force into modern criticism because he is a convenient peg on which to hang the disorderly and disintegrating materials which the Sackvilles and the Kyds could not quite straighten out.

These materials were the medieval systems of values, the inherited reasons for tragedy, the traditional meanings of tragedy. To trace these aspects of our subject we must take up our account once more in the Middle Ages.

5.

Tragedy in the hands of Boccaccio and Lydgate was an engulfing category. Therefore there is no real contradiction, I think, between the two divergent tendencies in *De Casibus* literature; the one, to regard a downfall as a visible punishment for specific sins; the other, to accept any downfall as evidence of the instability of all things here below. Where it is evident that the subject of the tragedy is a villain, the crimes themselves, as Lydgate says, cry out for divine vengeance and cause God to cast his eyes down and punish the sins. But when the protagonist has no conspicuous faults and yet undergoes a spectacular fall, such amazing reversals are to be expected too in a world which is only to be contemned and in which all that avails is the hope of better things hereafter; Boccaccio's beloved Pompey, upon whose dead body were heaped the most ghastly indignities that Boccaccio can imagine —great, noble, ill-fortuned Pompey—is Boccaccio's prime example. The first principle, that of direct punishment, floats around in this last all-inclusive principle. The first admits responsibility, but limits it to a mechanical, literal, eye-for-an-eye responsibility for crimes. The second denies responsibility and consequently precludes that sort of tragedy which arises, or appears to arise, out of the personal character of the individual human being. (I shall want later on to qualify to some extent the view, which seems to be implied here, that the Elizabethans wrote this sort of tragedy.) The two principles are not contradictory because, among intrinsically wicked men, the especially wicked may reap their especial punishments; but they are abstract, arbitrary, unwieldy, and therefore not conducive to great tragedy.

I labor these matters; for I think they are the double-gated entrance to the problem of Elizabethan tragedy. But they are not so clear cut in Boccaccio and Lydgate as I may seem to be indicating. The theory of omnipresent evil with its Contempt morality is modified on occasion, as it always had been, as by Thomas Aquinas to other ends in the preceding century for instance—is modified by Boccaccio to celebrate the noble worldly attainments of Pompey, though perhaps for the artistic reason of contrasting his fine eminence with his miserable fall, and is suspended significantly, as Professor Farnham describes, in the imposing "Defense of Alcibiades," in which Boccaccio makes a Renaissance apology for the life of heroic action. In fact, Boccaccio ends his great work by saying—I quote Professor Farnham:—

that one must love God, follow wisdom, and seek after the virtues. Also "seek honor, praise, and fame." (He lets that injunction stand without even a hint that he recognizes an inconsistency with his preachment *de contemptu mundi.*) If you do all these things you will show yourself worthy of the elevation which you achieve. "And if it should befall you to be hurled from your height, it would not appear to be because of your fault but rather because of the wantonness of Fortune, who is ever changing." [9]

Here the modification consists in this: the active life, if it is good, is most commendable, not the life of contempt of the world. Yet the world remains what it always was, insecure, ruled by the wanton, Fortune, and in this historically primary sense, evil. Thus Boccaccio's thought leads to a conception of peculiarly heroic conduct: be virtuously and eminently active, even though your activity must rest upon a foundation which is constantly crumbling, even though you may expect to fall through no responsibility of your own. [10] Such heroism, I think, moves up very close to the quality of Elizabethan tragedy. Needless to say, it is not stoicism; it is active while stoicism is passive, it is the opposite of an apartness from the world; and it is a firm, genuinely tragic attitude. It is also, so far as explicit statement goes, exceptional in Boccaccio's *De Casibus;* yet, once it comes out in the open, one wonders whether it had not been vitally implicit in many of the stories and whether the moralizings *de contemptu* have not been facile formulas.

The two divergent tendencies in medieval tragedy remain the same, whatever yearnings Boccaccio may have found in his heart to honor heroic activity: that downfall which is tragedy is the result either of manifest crime or of irresponsible mutability.

6.

It is in the growth and decay of these principles, and in the interplay between them, that English tragedy finds its being. All tragedy, I think it will be agreed, finds its particular being in its particular attitude towards the hard problem of retribution and responsibility on the one hand and in its particular illumination of the nature and place of man in the universe on the other hand; what these were in the first modern tragedies, we have just seen. What they came to a little later, in the sixteenth century, we shall now look into.

I am about to propound a theory which is not remarkably original in its general structure but which, since it takes rather abruptly an unusual turn, ought to be laid down here as a whole. This is it. Of the two tendencies in tragedy, that of giving examples of punishment for manifest sins outstripped the other. This development apparently marks a historical trend away from religious interests to cruder ethical interests. Then, with the enlargement of the scope of mechanical retribution, two things happened: everyday didacticism, with its untragic interest in the art of living successfully in the world, flourished as it had never flourished before; but the frequent arbitrary assignments of unfitting retributions, especially in cases where the crimes were not manifest, gave ostensibly didactic tragedies a decidedly sensational cast. At the same time the tendency to see tragedy as an illustration of the prevailing insecurity of the world had excellent representation; but the concomitant morality *de contemptu*, which grew dim in Boccaccio, faded out still more: the result is definite sensationalism. So —in simplest terms—tragedy became either narrowly didactic or irresponsibly sensational.

The unusual turn in this theory is the stress it puts on the sensationalism of tragic literature in the pre-Shakespearean period. The formulation describes this sensationalism as the result of the disintegration of the normal moral reasons for tragedy and of the inadequate conceptions of man's responsibility for his deeds. It is an estimate of the need for some thoroughgoing renovations in a sound but run-down structure.

In the first *Mirror for Magistrates* (1559) the stiff didactic intention predominates. The stories of the unhappy princes of Britain are told, William Baldwin says quite simply, to show how God deals with evil rulers:

> For here, as in a mirror or loking glasse, you shal se if any vice be found, how the like hath ben punished in other heretofore, whereby admonished, I trust it bee a good occasione to moue men to the soner amendment.[11]

So, in general and with qualifications presently to be noticed, the fallen worthies got themselves into their difficulties by persisting in sins like pride, treachery, envy, and carnal intemperance; the rationale of this is that men are responsible for their vices and therefore for their actions, that they can amend their characters and therefore their fortunes in this world. Thus the didacticism of *The Mirror.* Thus the plays like Gascoigne's *Glass of Government* and the huge "mirror" literature of the sixteenth century.

In the later drama the "domestic" tragedies, *Arden of Feversham* and *A Warning for Fair Women*, are the best illustrations of the arbitrary view that God's hand supports men when they are good and crushes them when they are bad. The husbands in these plays are thus supported supernaturally for a while, but when enough incriminating evidence is stacked against them, they are thrown headlong to their deaths; afterwards the veritable villains are also punished of course. Arden is guilty of avarice and sacrilege: abstract academic didacticism demands that if he is to suffer he must be unmistakably guilty. But Shakespearean tragedy will not be content with so simple a scheme of crime and punishment.

Nor was *The Mirror* fully. It displays, however, only an ability to skirt embarrassing problems. Where the connection between the sin and the retribution is not apparent, it falls back on rhetorical allusions to Fortune; where the presence of sin is doubtful, it manufactures a fault like "ambition," which, to be sure, approaches the status of a sin in the sixteenth century, but which, in view of the attendant plea to shun the world, must rather have stuck in the craws of the princes to whom *The Mirror* was addressed. Where the innocent have suffered, "haue for their vertue bin enuied and murdered," Baldwin makes a running leap over to the injunction, "be virtuous anyway," and God shall

eyther so maintaine you, that no malice shall preuaile, or if it do, it shal be for your good, and to your eternall glory both here and in heauen . . .

(*l. c.* p. 6)

Finally, *The Mirror*, in tracing the causes of tragedy back into faults of character, puts men on their own responsibility without asking whether the faults themselves are the effects of a deterministic system.

This is temporizing, but it looks in the right direction. Almost in spite of itself, *The Mirror* lets the tradition of fatal sins broaden out into a conception of tragic flaws. It puts necessary limits on the freedom of the will, and it acknowledges that much of the ill which happens to men cannot be explained by the theory of an ounce of punishment for an ounce of crime. So much to the good. The weakness—the sensationalism—results from the strained relationship between theory and event, from the rivalry of the glory of this world with the glory of heaven, and from the disproportion in spilling so much blood in order to enforce a usually pedestrian lesson in conduct. The weakness, needless to say, lay in the times in general rather than in *The Mirror* in particular.

7.

The two pieces which I shall venture to characterize as predominantly sensational are Thomas Churchyard's *Jane Shore* and Thomas Sackville's *Buckingham*, both of which appeared first in the extended *Mirror* of 1563. It happens, too, that these pieces are to be distinguished from the others on purely literary grounds; in comparison with Baldwin and Ferrers, Churchyard and Sackville are ardent in their devotion to clean versification and lively rhetoric, to an attractive display of the passions and to general literary effectiveness. This is enough to make them sensational if the meaning of their work is confused; that is to say, weak writing does not raise many questions because it does not arouse many feelings; whereas good writing, if it does not answer the questions it raises, becomes sensational.

The moot question here is that of confusion. In the first place it must be admitted that both Churchyard and Sackville are lavish givers of isolated didactic sentiments; the ghost of Jane Shore puts her reflections on chastity and modesty and generosity into many a wholesome phrase, and Buckingham sends pointed messages to kaiser, prince, and peer. But this is all by the way. Their complaints are directed not really against vice but against Fortune; their remonstrances aim not at the amendment of sin but at the avoidance of high place; their study is not to weigh this world against heaven but to proclaim the now measureless terror of the world. Change or insecurity, seen without reference to some stable principle, becomes terrible and sensational. The disorientation, the loss of the stable principle, is what I am calling confusion.

It is marked by a deliberate exploitation of conventional rhetoric. Churchyard is prolific in variations on this theme:

> This wandring world bewitched me with wiles,
> And won my wits, with wanton sugred ioyes:
> In Fortune's frekes, who trustes her when shee smiles,
> Shall finde her false, and full of fickle toyes . . .

Oh darke deceite, with painted face for sho,
Oh poysned bayte, that makes vs eger still,
Oh fayned frend, deceiuing people so,
Oh world, of thee, we cannot speake too ill:
Yet fooles wee are that bend so to thy skill:
The plague and scourge that thousands dayly feele
Should warne the wise to shun thy whirling wheele.

(*l. c.* II, 461–2; st. 2 & 4)

And Sackville cuts many stanzas for his tragedy from this same familiar piece of cloth. What has been lost in such rhetoric is final meaning; and the lost final meaning of the lines above can be recovered by turning back to similar earlier poetry, to, for instance, Skelton's *Edward IV*, which was included in the first edition of *The Mirror:*

Where was in my lyfe such one as I,
While lady fortune with me had continuaunce?
Graunted not shee mee to haue victory,
In *England* to rayne and to contribute *Fraunce?*
Shee tooke mee by the hand and led me a daunce,
And with her sugred lips on mee shee smyled;
But what for her dissembled countenaunce,
I could not beware till I was beguyled:
Now from this world shee hath mee exiled . . .

O lady *Bes* long for mee may you call,
For I am departed vntill dome's day:
But loue you that lord that is soueraine of all:
Where bee my castles and buildyngs royall?
But *Windsore* alone now I haue no moe,
And of *Eton* the prayers perpetuall,
Et ecce nunc in pulvere dormio.

(*l. c.* II, 245–6, st. 3 & 5)

The lost meaning is an actuating religious meaning. Nothing can show clearer the damage wrought by the loss than observation of the difference in feeling in these passages: Churchyard's polished and somewhat trite hysteria as against Skelton's lively and yet controlled sorrow. The loss in meaning makes Churchyard's rhetoric fall together with Seneca's; this means simply that the defacing of a common idea makes it indistinguishable, and that it can become distinguishable again only when it takes on new significance. That the significance of even Skelton's poem had faded out remarkably is indicated by the caption which the editors of *The Mirror* put above it: "Howe King *Edward* the fourth through his surfeting and vntemperate life, sodainly dyed in the middest of his prosperity." The religious significance is replaced thus by totally unjustified didacticism.

We are talking about an ultimate confusion in these pieces. This is not to say that they are confused in all respects or that they are so much empty rhetoric. *Buckingham* is brilliant, as we have said earlier, in its analysis of passion, and *Jane Shore* has some lyrical stanzas on love which I think have never been properly appreciated.[12] Both handle human beings in such an effective fashion that their great contribution to later literature is quite comprehensible. Both Sackville and Churchyard are doubtless entirely sincere in their dominant attitude that the world is unreliable and evil. Only the moral significance of these traditional attitudes is obscure.

8.

In *Gorboduc* the contributions of the two authors split the play into the kinds of didacticism and sensationalism which we have been describing. There is no need to repeat here our earlier remarks on Norton's engrossment with practical political morality, but we can now for the first time view Sackville's literary position fairly clearly. It looks very much like Churchyard's position and Sackville's own in *Buckingham*. Observe, for instance, that the attitude towards the world which lies behind the sensational events of Act IV is the same preoccupation with mutability:

> Your Grace should now in these graue yeres of yours
> Haue found ere this the price of mortall ioyes,
> How short they be, how fading here in earth,
> How full of chaunge, how brittle our estate,
> Of nothing sure saue onely of the death,
> To whom both man and all the world doth owe
> Their end at last.
>
> (IV, 2, 149–155)

And the moral import here is not Skelton's *In Manus tuas, Domine. . .* , but this:

> Neither should natures power
> In other sort against your hart preuaile
> Than as the naked hand whose stroke assayes
> The armed brest, where force doth light in vaine.
>
> (IV, 2, 155–158)

Stoicism, the reader will say. I should make no objection to the term except that it would seem to mean that sort of formal stoicism at which we were looking a few pages ago, and the sentiment expressed above, I think, is only generally and loosely stoical. It would be the natural result of shearing off the religious implications in the belief in an evil world, and, as such, it is another example of the momentary coincidence with broadly Senecan ethics.

More accurately, it is a coincidence with and a conscious adaptation of the general ethical attitudes of that whole body of classical literature to which scholarly poets had made an abrupt return. If we examine the classical allusions in *Gorboduc*, we shall find that there is none which points clearly and exclusively to a Senecan play and that each which has been asserted to be such an allusion must be traced to more imposing sources. The conspicuous allusions to the myth of Phaeton, for instance, have parallels in Seneca, but the great telling of the story, with suitable applications to the theme of the rashness of ambitious youth, is of course Ovid's, in the *Metamorphoses*, Book II; the stress on the indulgence of the parent, moreover, which comes out in the chorus to Act I, appears in Ovid's account but not in the Senecan passages. There are also, it happens, some lines in *Gorboduc* which illuminate the nature and the general origins of its "stoicism":

> "Oh, no man happie till his ende be seene."
> If any flowing wealth and seemyng ioye
> In present yeres might make a happy wight,
> Happie was Hecuba, the wofullest wretch

> That euer lyued to make a myrrour of;
> And happie Pryam with his noble sonnes . . .
>
> (III, 1, 11–16)

This might seem to be Senecan; but it is assuredly an allusion to the famous conversation between Solon and Croesus, which was reported by Herodotus and repeated by Plutarch. Happiness, Solon is said to have told Croesus, is not to be measured by wealth and power but by the possession of virtue, health, and good sons, and most importantly by the ability to die well. The story was reduced to the maxim, "Pronounce no man happy till he dies"; it was retold by Painter in *The Palace of Pleasure* (1564) and is referred to in *Titus Andronicus*:

> But safer triumph is this funeral pomp,
> That hath aspir'd to Solon's happiness,
> And triumphs over chance in honour's bed.
>
> (I, 1, 176–8)

The maxim was thus a favorite memento of chance, of the instability of human felicity, and being almost but not quite a *memento mori* it led not to religious faith but to a sort of classical discipline. The stoicism is not special; it is common to most ancient literature. It is, as yet, a somewhat clumsy substitute for theological Contempt of the World, and because it is clumsy, it contributes sensationalism to the literature of the pre-Shakespearean period. But its potentialities are great.

9.

The unresolved conflict between didacticism and sensationalism is striking in *Cambyses.* The title page and the prologue, the final speeches and the epilogue point the moral—that God (using an accident for his instrument) strikes down the evil ruler; but between these margins the scenes are replete with "wicked deedes and tyrannous murders," "plesant mirth," and "odious death." [13] Underneath this conflict in meaning or effect, there are others which are doubtless only cruder manifestations of the same conflict. According to the title page the play is a "lamentable tragedy," but the running title calls it a comedy; actually it is a mixture of tragedy, moral play, and comic interlude. In laying ostentatious claim upon ethical significance, it makes one of the few veritable references to Seneca, but it is as different from Senecan tragedy as day from night. It mixes piety with bombast, patriotism with horseplay. *Cambyses* shows better than any other piece the magnitude of the difficulties which the popular tragedy had to overcome—which is as much as saying that the popular tragedy will have attained a remarkable magnitude when it has overcome so many difficulties.

10.

The Misfortunes of Arthur (1588) overcame no difficulties. This youthful and overly ingenious work transforms one of the most celebrated pages in British legendary history into a pastiche of Senecanisms. Hence its interest to literary historians. It is also the supreme monument to confusion, the glaring example of the decay in English tragic processes. Lacking a specific didactic intention, it still maintains that men are responsible for their ills; "Humane Nature workes her dayly wrackes," says the epilogue,[14] and Arthur and Mordred were

> . . . both supprest and vanquisht by themselues.
>
> (Epil. 21)

So it is not God, not Fortune, nor any of the other medieval abstractions that moves the tragedy.

But instead of taking these failings in human nature seriously, instead of seeing a down-on-the-ground moral import in them, as did Baldwin and Norton, or instead of letting them lead to the genuine tragedy of the individual human being, as was begun at least by Churchyard and Sackville, the author proclaims responsibility and irresponsibility in one and the same breath:

> Such is the brittle breath of mortall man,
> Whiles humane *Nature* workes her daily wrackes:
> Such be the crazed crests of glorious Crownes,
> Whiles worldly powers like sudden puffes do passe.
>
> (Epil. 22–25)

Nor, after these aspersions upon worldly glory and power, does it help matters to find this sentiment expressed a few lines later:

> Swift is the tyme, wherein mans life doth run.
> But by his deedes t'extend renowme and fame,
> That onely vertue workes, which neuer fades.
>
> (Epil. 48–50)

The Misfortunes of Arthur is an unconscionable exploitation of the sensational features in the Senecan tragedies and the British myth. It is this and nothing more. I think that it marks the low ebb in tragedy because it shows, rather than a conflict in meaning or an imperfect meaning, no meaning at all.

II.

The recovery of meaning had already begun, however, in *The Spanish Tragedy*. The moral structure in Kyd's tremendously imaginative drama seems to be this:

In elemental terms, it can be said first of all to depict the wicked deeds and the just downfall of a villainous prince, Lorenzo. Thus it recapitulates the plan upon which were constructed the simplest metrical tragedies, and likewise *Cambyses*. The significance of the downfall, which had been religious at first and then had become arbitrary, now is given no specific expression. Add to this fact the multiplication of villains in the accomplices of Lorenzo, and the apparently unchecked sensationalism of the play is accounted for.

But it is really checked in a number of ways. As a counterpart to the pyramid of Lorenzo's rise and fall, there is the line of action given Hieronimo, which is motivated by reference to accepted schemes of ethical, worldly conduct: it is clear that Hieronimo, in his magisterial capacity, has some prerogatives as a public avenger.[15] They are in conflict with more powerful prerogatives and therefore lead to tragic consequences, but they justify his conduct; moreover, he resorts to them only when his appeals for unquestionable justice have utterly failed. So, although Hieronimo stirs our feelings much more than does Lorenzo, his rôle, to the extent that it makes ethical and moral sense, is not sensational. Hieronimo's rôle is not sensational in still another way: it makes psychological sense; it is real or understandable, and so is Isabella's. Kyd found the means of creating and communicating the suffering of these poor human beings so effectively that we cannot say how we should approve or disapprove of their actions; and thus he opened the way to genuine psychological tragedy.

For Hamlet is only a much more understandable Hieronimo. We watch while Hamlet labors to identify and to punish a murderer; we know the doubts, the impotent fury, the impulses, the hesitations, the sickness which his too-large task creates in him. This is the psychological stuff of Kyd's play raised to such a point that it dominates the whole of the tragic action; it is also very much refined. Titus Andronicus, who is created from the same stuff, is disappointing only because he is not raised above the level of Hieronimo. But the differences between these three tragic heroes are quantitative, I think, and not qualitative.

There is, of course, a vast difference between *Ham-*

let and *The Spanish Tragedy*. The former has a wholeness which the latter lacks; this, however, may well be due to the dominance of the rôle of the avenger. The former has a depth and a significance of which there are in the latter only meager germs. These are difficult quantities. Certainly the increased significance must go hand in hand with the increased stature of the human being, Hamlet, and is contingent upon his increased psychological reality; but Hamlet, the human being, does not exist *in vacuo*, and that vision which gave him his astounding stature must have been a vision of the world of human beings. There we must let the matter rest with only this negative observation: the significance of *Hamlet* quite obviously cannot be expressed in any simple formulas of responsibility and retribution, nor can it be measured by any of the usual moral and ethical standards. No more can *King Lear* or *Othello*. But if we grant that Hamlet, though he is complex, is still thoroughly understandable, and that because we understand him and because we are given no clue to definite evil in him, we do not turn our moral condemnation against him—then, with a gesture of gratitude towards Kyd, we can say that the English tragedy is freed from empty sensationalism, and we are ready to accept any convincing description of its moral significance.

The historically fundamental structure in *The Spanish Tragedy*, as we have said, is the pyramid of Lorenzo's rise and fall. In comparison with it the story of Hieronimo was an engraftment which flourished so well that it practically obscured the original trunk. The original trunk is there, nevertheless; it reproduces the form of the simple metrical tragedies and, with the addition of psychological reality again, *Richard III* and *Macbeth*. Lorenzo's pyramid, moreover, fits into the whole tragic composition just exactly as do those of Aaron, Claudius, and Edmund. We can now do a little plain sailing in our exploration of ethical principles: villainous characters, whether they are Cambyses, Richard III, or Macbeth, or Lorenzo, Aaron, Claudius, or Edmund, are all subject to an invariable retribution for evil; they are punished for their vices as flatly and as forthrightly as any William Baldwin could ask. In this the great tragedy clings to a central dogma of the metrical tragedy.

There are changes, to be sure. God is no longer visible as the arm of punishment; abstract didacticism is abandoned; the connections between vice and death are vital rather than arbitrary. This is much the same as saying that the evil characters, like the ones who are not clearly evil, are understandable and make their own psychological sense. Consequently we can and do often feel sympathy with them. But we condemn them nevertheless, and our condemnation must be a reflection of a clear-cut ethical system which refuses always to allow evil to flourish.

In *The Spanish Tragedy* psychological truth is confined to Hieronimo and Isabella. Otherwise the tragedy is another dark picture of a violently unstable world; here, as in Churchyard's and Sackville's narrative work, the unstability is formless, directionless, and sensational; it is seen in reference to no clear principle, neither in reference to religious faith nor to stoicism. Being undistinguished thus, it receives an undistinguished expression, which coincides with Senecan rhetoric sometimes or occasionally, as in III, 1—

> So striueth not the waues with sundry winds
> As fortune toyleth in the affaires of kings. . . . 3

—derives directly from the Senecan tragedies. In so far as Kyd is the slave of rhetoric he illustrates the plight in which writers in general were left by the disintegration of medieval philosophy.

Kyd and his contemporaries and his predecessors were learning only slowly what to do about all the evil that they saw around them in the world. Sackville had begun to discover that passion was worth detailed analysis and that a passionate outcry for vengeance merited the utterance. Kyd found out that the suffering which sheerly wicked people cause in others was a tremendous field to explore, and he invented the means to that end. Shakespeare continued in these new directions.

And so there came about a renovation in the motives of tragedy, which consisted in, I think, a recasting of the Contempt of the World attitude. In a sense this new comprehension was literary, idea-istic, and somewhat comparable with Montaigne's thought, instinctively drawing, as did Montaigne's thought, on general Roman classicism. But it seems to have gone very deep, and to have been thoroughly lived out at least in the artistic life. It was founded on these venerable propositions: the world is evil, all appearances deceive, change is continuous and (from our modern point of view) irrational, youth is by nature irresponsible, human institutions are finally negligible.

The general manner of human failure can be realized in retrospective, analytical, cause-and-effect terms; but at the same time fate ultimately overrules all. The superb heroic figures that are studied in tragedy combat the evil world, but they are regularly overcome by it; and their greatness is always inscrutably vitiated, for they are a part of the world. In this situation there is a split and an antagonism between human responsibility for tragic deeds and the responsibility of the evil world; here the interplay of the metrical tragedy's idea of personal guilt and punishment, with the sensational, rhetorical tragedy's idea of Fortune, is apparent. Shakespeare's interest, especially in *Hamlet*, seems to be directly in the sparks cast off by these clashing views.

All this does not quite add up to a paradox. For we can say that we have freedom of choice and responsibility for our actions, and retrospectively we can see our wrong choices. But our freedom exists of course only within limits, and in the tragic situation, which is the most important and typical of situations, the limits are so constricted as to be removed.

Out of this seems to come a moral philosophy, not of stoicism, but of a sober and quite unspectacular heroism. Shakespeare, like Boccaccio, seems to be saying, be virtuously and eminently active, even though your activity must rest on a foundation which is constantly crumbling, even though you may expect to fall through no responsibility of your own. Heroically noble characters achieve poise but no assurance against outrageous misfortune, and in the end only understanding of, and compassion for, the human predicament avail.

NOTES

(In quoting Shakespeare I have used the Oxford text in one volume, ed. W. J. Craig, 1928.)

NOTES TO THE INTRODUCTION

1. In tying tragic technique together with moral significance and in looking for excellence in both, I am perhaps flying in the face of a favorite dogma in the later criticism and am at the same time apparently ranging myself with the moralistic criticism of the past century, which was, as everyone knows, often ludicrous. Explanations are not easy here; possibly I can suggest the general nature of my convictions by borrowing a key sentence or two from the criticism of one of my contemporaries, Yvor Winters. I think, for instance, that "if the poetic discipline is to have steadiness and direction, it requires an antecedent discipline of ethical thinking and of at least some ethical feeling, which may be in whole or in part the gift of religion or social tradition, or which may be largely the result of individual acquisition by way of study" (Yvor Winters, *Primitivism and Decadence*, New York, 1937). This means, for me, two things: first, that there is what Mr. Winters calls "a common moral territory" in which all good art is rooted, for "the fundamental concepts of morality are common to intelligent men" regardless of such individual orientations as the theological; and secondly, that a deliberate and sound cultivation of this common moral territory, that conscious philosophy in other words, is *not* necessary to the poet but is always a tremendous advantage to him, other felicities in his work being equal.
2. *Shakespeare's Philosophical Patterns* (Baton Rouge, La., 1937).
3. *Elizabethan Critical Essays*, ed. G. G. Smith (Oxford, 1904), II, 316.
4. Ed. Joseph Haslewood (London, 1815), I, 153.
5. Cunliffe, *op. cit.*, p. lxviii.
6. (Cambridge, Mass., 1936), pp. 68–9.

7. *Technique of the Drama* (Chicago, 1895), p. 2.
8. *Shakespearean Tragedy* (London, 1932), p. 9. The first edition appeared in 1904.

NOTES TO CHAPTER I

Gorboduc: Some Fundamental Problems in the Early Dramatic Tragedy

1. The printer's note to the edition of 1570, reprinted in *Chief Pre-Shakespearean Dramas*, ed. J. Q. Adams (Boston, 1924), p. 503: the text cited hereafter.
2. *Apologie for Poetrie*, ed. Edward Arber (London, 1929), p. 63.
3. ". . . *Gorboduck* is a fable, doubtless, better turn'd for Tragedy, than any on this side the Alps in his time; and might have been a better direction to Shakespear and Ben. Johnson than any guide they have had the luck to follow.

   "Here is a King, the Queen, and their two Sons. The King divides his Realm, and gives it betwixt his two Sons. They quarrel. The Elder Brother Kills the Younger. Which provokes the Mother to Kill the Elder. Thereupon the King Kills the Mother. And then to make a clear Stage the people rise and dispatch old Gorboduck.

   "It is objected by our Neighbors against the English, that we delight in bloody spectacles. Our Poets who have not imitated *Gorboduck* in regularity and roundness of the design, have not failed on the Theatre to give us the *atrocité* and blood, enough in all Conscience." Thomas Rymer, *A Short View of Tragedy* (London, 1693), pp. 84–5. Rymer appears to have deviated from the fable for the sake of climax. Actually the people kill both the king and queen.
4. *Biographia Britannica* (London, 1747), pp. 3543 ff.
5. F. E. Schelling, *Elizabethan Drama* (Boston, 1908), II, 401; A. W. Ward, *A History of English Dramatic Literature* (London, 1899); H. Schmidt, "Seneca's Influence upon *Gorboduc*," *Modern Language Notes*, II (1887), 2, pp. 28–35; J. W. Cunliffe, *The Influence of Seneca on Elizabethan Tragedy* (London, 1893).
6. L. H. Courtney, "Ferrex and Porrex," *Notes and Queries*, ser. 2, X, pp. 261–3; L. Toulmin Smith (ed.), *Gorboduc*, Englische Sprach-und-Literaturdenkmale des 16. 17. und 18. Jhrhts (Heilbronn, 1883); S. A. Small, "The Political Import of the Norton Half of *Gorboduc*," *PMLA*, XLVI (1931), 3.

7. Schelling, *l. c.*
8. Courtney, *l. c.*
9. H. A. Watt, *Gorboduc; or, Ferrex and Porrex* (Bulletin of the University of Wisconsin, No. 351 [1910]). The substance of this study is to be found in Professor Watt's notes on *Gorboduc*, in *Early English Classical Tragedies*, ed. J. W. Cunliffe (Oxford, 1912), pp. 297–307.
10. Thomas Warton, *History of English Poetry* (London, 1871), IV, 266.
11. Cf. Watt, *op. cit.*, pp. 19 ff.
12. Cf. Watt, p. 29. The assignment is made in a note to Harvey's copy of Gascoigne's *Jocasta*, ed. J. W. Cunliffe, p. 420; and in a letter to Spenser, ed. G. G. Smith, I, 126.
13. In Harvey's letter to Spenser.
14. See the present writer, "Some Blank Verse Written By Thomas Norton before *Gorboduc*," *Modern Language Notes*, December, 1933, pp. 529–30.
15. The P[rinter] to the Reader, *l. c.* (See note 1 *supra.*)
16. Watt, *op. cit.*, p. 30.
17. F. Koch, "*Ferrex und Porrex;* eine literarhistorische Untersuchung," Jahres-Bericht der Realschule zu Altona über das Schuljahr 1880–1, No. I, pp. i–xvii.
18. Examples of repetition of words in *Gorboduc:*

Read, read, my lordes . . .	III, 1, 27
Once, once haue hapt . . .	IV, 1, 9
Thou, Porrex, thou . . .	IV, 1, 29
	—etc.

Examples of repetition in Norton's Psalms:

And that thou, thou hast done it . . .	Psalm 109
Against thee, thee alone . . .	51
Thy servant, Lord, thy servant, lo . . .	116
Arise, O Lord, arise I say . . .	132
. . . depart, depart from me I say.	139
	—etc.

19. See pp. 63–7 *infra.*
20. Koch, *op. cit.*, p. vi.
21. Cf. I, 1, 59 ff.:

When lordes, and trusted rulers vnder kinges,
To please the present fancie of the prince,
With wrong transpose the course of gouernance,

> Murders, mischiefe, or ciuill sword at length . . .
> Bringes them to cruell and reprochfull death . . .

and V, 1, 41–45.

22. I submit lines from V, 2, with a few italics to indicate the cruxes:

> And thou, O Brittaine, whilome in renowme, 229
> Thus wasted and defaced, spoyled and destroyed! 232
> This is the end when in fonde princes hartes
> Flattery preuailes, and sage rede hath no place. 236–7
> And this doth growe when, loe, vnto the prince
> Whom death or sodeine happe of life bereaues
> No certaine heire remaines—such certaine heire
> As not all-onely is the rightfull heire
> *But to the realme is so made knowen to be* . . . 246–50
>
> No, no; then *Parliament should haue bene holden*
> *And certeine heires appointed to the crowne* . . . 264–5
> While yet the prince did liue, whose name and power
> By lawfull sonmons and authoritie
> Might make a Parliament to be of force . . . 268–70
> In which your Parliament, and in your choise,
> Preferre the right my lordes . . . 160–1
> Right meane I his or *hers* vpon whose name
> The people rest by meane of natiue line
> Or by vertue of *some former lawe*,
> Already made their title to aduance.
> Such one, my lordes, let be your chosen king,
> Such one, *so borne within your natiue land*,
> Such one preferre. 164–71

23. In *The Mirror for Magistrates*, ed. Joseph Haslewood (London, 1815), II: At the end of the poem.
24. *Biographia Britannica, l. c.*
25. Stanza 61 (Haslewood, II, 349). Cf. also St. 71. The fact that these sentiments in *Gorboduc* are expressed by a dramatic character qualifies them in no way: Eubulus is the good counsellor throughout the play. Cp. these lines with II, 1, 143–5, where scorn of *rascal routs* is bitterly satirized; and cf. *infra* pp. 35–8.
26. Cf. V, 2, 269; and note 22 *supra.*
27. Calvin, *The Institutes* (London, 1562), p. 502 *verso.*
28. Note, however, the violent construction put upon inaction in

Norton's oration on the subject (cf. pp. 28–9 *infra*), and also the language of V, 2.

29. Although these poems were not printed until 1563, in the second edition of *The Mirror*, the fore-link which introduces them, the fact that Sackville wrote an "induction" intended for a series of tragedies and the fact that in the *Induction* he writes:

    My busie minde presented unto mee
    Such fall of pieres as in this realme had be:
    That ofte I wisht some would their woes descryve
    To warne the rest whom fortune left alive.
    (St. 10)

    —would seem to indicate that Sackville began work on tragedies before interest in tragical literature crystallized into *The Mirror*. The first edition of *The Mirror* appeared in 1559.
30. Reprinted by Haslewood in his introduction to *The Mirror*.
31. Roger Ascham, *The Scholemaster*, ed. Edward Arber (London, 1895), p. 71.
32. *Biographia Britannica, l. c.*; Holinshed's *Chronicles*, year 1570/1.
33. *Biographia Britannica, l. c.*
34. Quoted by E. K. Chambers, *The Elizabethan Stage* (Oxford, 1923), IV, 273.
35. William Cobbet, *The Parliamentary History of England* . . . (London, 1806), I, 695. I identify the petition quoted in the text above by combining the references in the various editions of the Commons Journals. With lines 8–12 above compare *Gorboduc* V, 2, 227–33:

    The townes shall be consumed and burnt with fire,
    The peopled cities shall waxe desolate;
    And thou, O Brittaine, whilome in renowme,
    Whilome in wealth and fame, shalt thus be torne,
    Dismembred thus, and thus be rent in twaine,
    Thus wasted and defaced, spoyled and destroyed:
    These be the fruites your ciuil warres will bring.

    With lines 15–20 compare *Gorboduc* V, 2, 153–6 and 195–7:

    If ye shall all with one assent forbeare
    Once to lay hand or take vnto your-selues
    The crowne by colour of pretended right
    Or by what other meanes so-euer it be . . .

And who will not by force attempt to winne
So great a gaine, that hope perswades to haue?
A simple colour shall for title serue.

Cp. 7 and 21–3 with *Gorboduc* V, 2, 176–9:

With that same hart, my lordes, keepe out also
Unnaturall thraldome of strangers reigne,
Ne suffer you against the rules of kinde
Your mother land to serue a forreine prince.

—and note how sharply both are directed against Mary Stuart.

36. S. A. Small in one of the most recent studies of *Gorboduc*—"The Political Import of the Norton Half of *Gorboduc*," *PMLA*, XLVI (1931), No. 3—accepts Griffith's division of the play without question. The conclusions of this study are as follows:

> "Thomas Norton, the staunch puritan, naturally chose in his half of the play (the first three acts) to emphasize, principally through the counselors, the moral lesson that rulers should obey the good advice of their statesmen on matters pertaining to the welfare of the kingdom. This would very naturally prepare the mind of the Queen for Sackville's argument for the limitation of the succession which is presented in the fifth act." (p. 641.)

This article rests on the fallacy which Watt pointed out in the work of F. Koch: "Koch makes a slip in logic . . . in believing that the three-fold repetition of the allusion to Phaeton in the first two acts, while the story is not referred to in the last two acts, is an indication of Sackville's authorship of Acts IV and V; with the end of the third act, the practical need of the story was over; there was in the last two acts no demand for such an illustration." (Watt, *l. c.*, p. 30.) Similarly, after King Gorboduc has proceeded to definite action, there is *no demand* for stressing the importance of good advice; and actually good advice is stressed in the second part, e.g., in V, 2, 236–7 (see note 22 *supra*), etc. But the reverse of this situation is more importantly true: while Gorboduc and his heirs are living there could not possibly be "an argument for the limitation of the succession." And, as all the historical critics have observed, it is the final scene of the play which contains the natural appeal of the staunch puritan—i.e., the appeal for Lady Katharine Grey.

37. Schmidt, *l. c.;* Watt, *op. cit.*, pp. 68 ff.

38. I have retained Watt's readings and enumerations of the Senecan text.

39. Thomas Sternhold and John Hopkins, *The Whole Booke of Psalmes, Collected into English Meeter* (London, 1616).

40. Watt follows Schmidt in these tests. Compare the diction in the following lines from Norton's Psalms:

    Therefore now, all ye bloody men . . . Ps. 139

    He turned their waters into blood . . . 105

    Whose subtil mouth of vanity
      with flattering words do threat,
    And their right hand is a right hand
      of guile and subtilty. 144

    But in their tents with grudging heart
      they wickedly repine. 106
    —etc.

41. Watt, *op. cit.*, p. 58.

42. This legend, as in the Middle Ages, connects English with classical history, and it is in *Gorboduc* quite unmistakably a motivation for the classicism. This is rather clearly indicated, I think, by some lines which occur earlier in the play:

    . . . if the mindfull wrath of wrekefull gods,
    Since mightie Ilions fall not yet appeased
    With these poore remnantes of the Troian name,
    Haue not determined by vnmoued fate
    Out of this realme to rase the Brittishe line . . .
    (II, 2, 75–9)

43. The *Induction*, because of its Virgilian and generally classical imagery, appears also to be more Senecan than is Seneca himself; e.g.:

    When I beheld the wofull werd befall,
    That by the wrathful wyl of Gods was come:
    And Jove's unmooved sentence and foredome
    On Priam kyng . . . (St. 63)

    Sorrowe I am, in endles tormentes payned,
    Among the furies in the infernall lake:

> Where Pluto god of hel so griesly blacke
> Doth hold his throne, and Letheus deadly taste
> Doth rieve remembraunce of eche thyng fore past. (St. 16)

See also pp. 85–6 *infra.*

44. Lydgate, *Fall of Princes*, ed. Henry Bergen (E.E.T.S., 1924), Bk. III, 1, 890 ff.
45. L. H. Courtney (*l. c.*) pointed out that these lines are an exact counterpart to the conclusion of an oration, probably by Norton, on the succession, given in the House of Commons, Jan. 16, 1562/3:

    If we shall for any affection take away the right from those who have the right, let us remember this saying of the Holy Ghost, 'Propter injurias et injustitias transfertur regnum a Gente in Gentem.'
46. *Agam.*, 264 and 269–72:

    > Ignota tibi sunt jura regnorum aut nova.
    > Nobis maligni judices, aequi sibi,
    > Id esse regni maximum pignus putant,
    > Si quidquid aliis non licet, solis licet.

    With this Watt compares *Gorboduc* I, 2, 262–6; III, Ch. 1–3; and (incompletely) II, 1, 143–55 (to be quoted immediately above).
47. *Newton's Seneca*, ed. T. S. Eliot (New York, 1927), II, 112:

    > The subtil science of the law,
    > the statutes of our land,
    > (That long agoe decreed were)
    > thou dost not understand.
    > The Judges be malicious men,
    > they spyght and envye us,
    > But he shal have them partiall
    > his causes to discus.
    > This is the chiefest priviledge
    > that doth to Kinges belong.
    > What lawes forbiddeth other men,
    > they doe, and doe no wronge.
48. Watt, *l. c.*, pp. 67, 72, and 34.
49. *The Complaint of Henry Duke of Buckingham*, ed. Marguerite Hearsey (New Haven, 1936), p. 92.
50. *Ibid.*, p. 115. The relevant passages from *Buckingham* and *Gorboduc* are quoted on p. 22 *supra.*

51. Cf. Wilson, *Arte of Rhetorique* (Oxford, 1909), p. 7 with, e.g., *Gorboduc* I, 2, 247–336 (Eubulus' oration).
52. For a discussion of the chorus and *nuntius* see Chapter III, pp. 141 and 144 ff. *infra.*
53. Sackville uses the word as a comparative:

    For noble bloud made me both prince and peere,
    Yea peereless too . . . (*Buckingham*, St. 3)

    For examples in Norton's work see any of his psalms, including the excerpt quoted p. 31 *supra.*
54. Other mannerisms of Norton seem to include the use of *also* at the end of a rhetorical period or a line of verse, and the use of the expression *I say;* see note 18 *supra*, and p. 28 *supra*, the petition, line 5.
55. "A Type of Blank Verse Line Found in the Earlier Elizabethan Drama," *PMLA*, XXXII, No. 1.
56. *Piers Plowman* was not printed until 1550, but in 1550 Robert Crowley printed three impressions of it.
57. Quoted by L. Toulmin Smith, *op. cit.*, p. xxviii.
58. Quoted by Cooper, *op. cit.*, p. xxxix.
59. A tabulation of the Norton type of balanced line is as follows:
    I, 2: lines 9 86 91 100 102 104 128 170 175 189 215 225 292 316 320 354; and doubtless others like 105 109 191 246 260 etc.
    II, 1: lines 15 19 32 33 39 62 82 92 103 124 167 169 196 206 208.
    II, 2: lines 23 57 75 (this is a very short scene).
    III: lines 12 21 33 36 39 74 117 140 142 149.
    V, 2: lines 25 27 29 30 49 89 111 120 137 141 172 177 182 277.

    Of this type of line there are one or two examples in the first scene of the play (line 7, but scarcely line 2 in view of the enjambement); one or two in IV, 1 (16 and ?17 and ?19); five (18, 21, 108, 186, and 229) in the extensive IV, 2; two or three in V, 1 (59, ?23 and ?147).
60. Note that this is a balanced line, like those characteristic of Norton, but that in its context it is a part of a highly complicated, run-on movement.
61. See p. 82 ff. *infra.*

NOTES TO CHAPTER II

The Formation of the Heroic Medium

1. E.g.; Arnold Schröer, "Uber die Anfänge des Blankverses in England," *Anglia*, IV (1881), 1–72; Joseph B. Mayor, *Chapters*

on English Meter (London, 1901); J. Schipper, *Englische Metrik* (Bonn, 1888); George Saintsbury, *A History of English Prosody* (London, 1906); Paul Verrier, *Les Principes de la Métrique Anglaise* (Paris, 1909); C. E. Andrews, *The Writing and Reading of Verse* (New York, 1918).

2. I am convinced of the especial value of a general work on the poetry of this period: W. J. Courthope, *A History of English Poetry* (London, 1897), vol. II.
3. "It is I think justifiable to speak of these poets—Marlowe, Peele, Greene, Lodge, Nashe, Kyd, and others more dimly discerned—as a school. They worked in collaboration and interchanged their praises. They have a common bond in classical knowledge and the attempt to conquer the popular stage for literature. . . . The analysis of style must go a good deal further before it is possible to lay a finger on any passage of a play of the early 'nineties and say with confidence, 'This is Marlowe,' or 'This is Greene,' or 'This is the young Shakespeare.' " E. K. Chambers, "The Unrest in Shakespeare Studies," *The Nineteenth Century*, 101 (1927), 255–60.
4. *Studies in Philology*, XIX (1922), 186–205.
5. Professor Brooke reprints the relevant passage.
6. Cf. Lytton Strachey, *Pope* (New York, 1936), p. 22 ff. But in this regard the lines of the player-king in *Hamlet* are not without interest; e.g.:

   Most necessary 'tis that we forget
   To pay ourselves what to ourselves is debt;
   What to ourselves in passion we propose,
   The passion ending, doth the purpose lose.

   —etc.

7. Jasper Heywood, "To the Reader," *Troas*, in *Newton's Seneca*, ed. T. S. Eliot (New York, 1927), II, 4.
8. All quotations from Marlowe are from *The Works of Christopher Marlowe*, ed. C. F. Tucker Brooke (Oxford, 1910).
9. Prefatory to *Perimedes the Blacksmith* (1588).
10. Prefatory to *Menaphon* (1589).
11. *Idem.*
12. Prefatory to *The Groat's Worth of Wit* (1592).
13. In this connection the title page of the new, blank verse version of *Tancred and Gismund* (1591) is significant: "Newly revised and polished according to the decorum of these days."
14. Cf. *NED.*

15. Van Dam and Stoffel hold doubtless too closely to the principle of the strictly decasyllabic line; they are led to maintain that variations are corruptions. Cf., e.g., *Chapters on English Printing, Prosody, and Pronunciation* (Heidelberg, 1902). But both the general principle and the works of these critics are important; cf. also B. A. P. Van Dam, "Marlowe's *Tamburlaine*," *English Studies*, Feb. and Apr., 1934.
16. See pp. 41–4 *supra* and Chapter I, note 55.
17. See p. 34 *supra.*
18. These remarks have implications. If we accept Clarence's prayer as an expression of literary convention, then we can overcome several perplexing problems. The question why this scene is, in Shakespeare, so unusually heavy in Christian theology, and how it can shift so lightly from serious to frivolous theology, becomes a question of little moment. (Similarly, if Tamburlaine is a variation on convention, then he is not very good evidence of Marlowe's atheism.) I do not mean wholly to subscribe to Professor E. E. Stoll's theories: a poet's morality is to be found in wholes, not in lines and passages, and discussion of wholes cannot be attempted here.
19. Cf. A. K. Foxwell, *A Study of Sir T. Wyatt's Poems* (London, 1911).
20. *The Poems of Henry Howard, Earl of Surrey*, ed. F. M. Padelford (Seattle, 1928), Bk. II, 21.
21. *The Poetical Works of Gavin Douglas*, ed. John Small (Edinburgh, 1874), vol. II, Bk. II, 4.
22. *Newton's Seneca*, II, 6.
23. *Ibid.*, p. 4.
24. It is possible that Heywood is following Sackville's *Induction*, and that Sackville was following Surrey. If so, the *Induction* was then available in manuscript form earlier than 1559; cf. Ch. I, note 29.
25. *The Mirror for Magistrates*, ed. Haslewood, II, 327.
26. *The Heroycall Epistles*, ed. F. S. Boas (London, 1928), p. 226.
27. Cf. F. M. Padelford (ed.), *The Poems of Henry Howard* . . .
28. Thomas Phaer, *The Nyne fyrst Bookes of The Eneidos*. . . . (London, 1562).
29. *The Complete Works of George Peele*, ed. A. H. Bullen (London, 1888); "The Honour of the Garter," l. 55 (II, 319).
30. The Prologue to Book IV.
31. *Tottel's Miscellany* (*1557–1587*), ed. Hyder Edward Rollins (Cambridge, Mass., 1928), I, 120.

32. Cf. *The Complete Works of Geoffrey Chaucer*, ed. F. N. Robinson (Boston, 1933), p. 783; l. 2601 ff. Some of the lines in the comparable passages are these:

Gautier (Migne's *Patrologia Latina*, vol. 209; Bk. III, l. 1263 ff.):

Seminat in Persas lethi genus omne, cruentas
Excutuens Bellona manus; gemit ille recluso
Gutture, trajecto jacet ille per ilia ferro:
Hunc sparus exanimat, hunc tundit funda . . .

Grimald follows Gautier's syntax:

Shaking her bloody hands, Bellone, among
The Perses, soweth all kindes of cruel death.
With throte ycutt, hee roores: hee lyeth along,
His entrails with a launce through girded quite:
Him smites the club, him wounds farstryking bowe . . .

But Chaucer had used similar syntax (*The Knight's Tale*, l. 2612 ff.):

He thurgh the thikkeste of the throng gan threste;
Ther stomblen steedes stronge, and doun gooth al;
He rolleth under foot as dooth a bal;
He foyneth on his feet with his tronchoun,
And he hym hurtleth with his hors adoun;
He thurgh the body is hurt and sithen take . . .

And compare *The Legend of Good Women*, 635 ff.

33. *Tottel's Miscellany*, I, 115. I use in part the readings of the second edition, also of 1557.

34. *The Works of Thomas Kyd*, ed. F. S. Boas (Oxford, 1901).

35. *Ibid.*, Introduction.

36. *Oeuvres Complètes de Robert Garnier*, ed. L. Pinvert (Paris, 1923), I, 157:

Bellonne, ardant de rage, au plus fort de la presse
Couroit qui ça qui là, d'une prompte allégresse,
Détranchoit, terrassoit, faisoit sourdre un estang
Ou passoit son espée ointe de nostre sang.

37. Cf. A. McL. Witherspoon, *The Influence of Robert Garnier on Elizabethan Drama* (Yale Studies, LXV [1924]). This work includes an excellent survey of the background of Garnier and of the relevant scholarship.

38. This and the paragraphs immediately following are rewritten from my note, "Some Blank Verse Written by Thomas Norton Before *Gorboduc*," *Modern Language Notes*, Dec., 1933.
39. The P[rinter] to the Reader, John Day's edition of *Gorboduc*, 1570.
40. *The Poetical Works of Sir David Lyndsay*, ed. David Laing (Edinburgh, 1879).
41. The Prologue to Book VII; Douglas' *Works*, III, 75. Sackville's introductory stanzas also resemble other medieval poems. Cf. Marguerite Hearsey's edition of the poem (*op. cit.*, pp. 93–4).
42. The opening speech of Videna has been compared with *Hercules Furens* 125–40, *Oedipus* 1–5, *Agamemnon* 53–6, and *Octavia* 1–6. Why I think that Videna's lines are not "distinctly Senecan in style" (H. E. Watt), the reader has seen; that they reproduce some Senecan imagery is clear, but that it is distinctly and exclusively Senecan imagery is very doubtful.
43. In this connection we might notice some of Gavin Douglas' rhetoric:

    Pluto, thow patron of the deip Acheron,
    Fadir of turmentis in thine infernale see,
    Amid the fludis Stix and Flegiton,
    Lethe, Cochite, the wateris of oblivie,
    With dolorus quhirling of furious sisteris thre,
    Thyne now sal be my muse and drery sang;
    To follow Virgile in this dirk poese,
    Convey me, Sibill, that I ga nocht wrang.
    (Prologue to Bk. VI of the *Aeneid*)

    Miss Hearsey also compares the passages in question with Douglas, and with Lydgate as well (*op. cit.*, pp. 98 and 108).
44. See pp. 41 ff. *supra*.
45. A. C. Sprague (ed.), *Samuel Daniel/Poems and A Defence of Ryme* (Cambridge, Mass., 1930), pp. xvi and xviii.
46. *The Complete Works of George Gascoigne*, ed. J. W. Cunliffe (Cambridge, 1907 and 1910). The play is called a "moral discourse" by Gascoigne in his prefatory epistle (I, 13); and both morality and Euripides are insisted on by the printer (Quarto 1, 1573: Cunliffe, I, 476).
47. A useful analysis of Gascoigne's rhetoric in *Jocasta* is contained in Richard Henning's *George Gascoigne als Ubersetzer italienischer Dichtungen* (Königsberg, 1913); Henning calls the

sensational clichés "Surreyisms," but I doubt that they can be ascribed so directly to a single literary influence.

48. *The Heroycall Epistles*, ed. F. S. Boas.
49. Brooke, "Marlowe's Versification and Style," *Studies in Philology*, XIX (1922), p. 188.
50. *Idem.*
51. *Ibid.*, p. 187.
52. I draw this conclusion from Padelford's bibliography, and from A. W. Pollard and G. R. Redgrave, *A Short-Title Catalogue* (London, 1926). The matter is worth mentioning because Professor Brooke's remark has misleading implications.
53. In a less extensive way, Marlowe did something similar. It is notable, too, that he uses the Troy story as a metaphor to describe Zenocrate's beauty:

    And had she liu'd before the siege of *Troy*,
    Hellen, whose beauty sommond Greece to armes,
    And drew a thousand ships to Tenedos,
    Had not bene man'd in *Homers* Iliads . . .

    (*Tamb.* 3055 ff.)

NOTES TO CHAPTER III

The Spanish Tragedy, *Titus Andronicus*, AND SENECANISM

1. The first part of this chapter is reproduced with minor changes from my article, "Ghosts and Guides: Kyd's *Spanish Tragedy* and the Medieval Tragedy," *Modern Philology*, XXXIII (1935), 27–35.
2. *The Influence of Seneca on Elizabethan Tragedy* (London, 1893).
3. F. S. Boas (ed.), *The Works of Thomas Kyd* (Oxford, 1901), p. xxxii.
4. F. L. Lucas, *Seneca and Elizabethan Drama* (Cambridge, 1922).
5. T. S. Eliot (ed.), *Newton's Seneca* (New York, 1927), p. xxiv.
6. Boas, *op. cit.*, p. xxxiii.
7. *Ibid.*, p. xxxii.
8. *The Mirror for Magistrates*, ed. Haslewood; "The Complaint of the Duke of Buckingham," st. 93.
9. It is possible that Sackville found suggestion for the revenge motif in Virgil; at least Buckingham is remarkably parallel with Deiphobus: both are given gruesome descriptions, both tell a tale of betrayal, and both ask for vengeance.

10. *The Fall of Princes*, ed. Henry Bergen (London, 1924), Bk. VI. Note especially the description of Pompey (VI, 918–43).
11. *The Spanish Tragedy*, IV, 2, 24 ff. Cf. pp. 98 ff. *supra.*
12. There is such a narrative in *Hercules Furens* III, 2. It is, however, not notably Senecan, it has no connection with ghosts, and it is not a part of the "machinery" of the drama.
13. *Span. Trag.*, Induction l. 78 ff.
14. Cf. pp. 144 ff. *infra.*
15. Among the studies of which I am thinking but which I shall not mention later are the following:

    A. W. Ward, *History of English Dramatic Literature* (London, 1899), 2 vols.; A. H. Thorndike, *Tragedy* (Boston, 1908); F. E. Schelling, *Elizabethan Drama, 1558–1642* (Boston, 1908), 2 vols.; C. F. Tucker Brooke, *The Tudor Drama* (Boston, *c.* 1911); Harriot E. Fansler, *The Evolution of Technic in Elizabethan Tragedy* (Chicago, 1914).

    On the other hand some of the older studies have presented better balanced accounts of the development of English tragedy, e.g., Rudolph Fischer, *Zur Kunstentwicklung der Englischen Tragödie* (Strassburg, 1893). And there is at least one work which is exceptional in this field: Frank Louis Schoel, *Etudes sur l'Humanisme Continental en Angleterre à la Fin de la Renaissance* (Paris, 1926); this work shows that much of Chapman's so-called Senecanism is derived directly from Renaissance sources.
16. Emile Legouis and Louis Cazamian, *A History of English Literature* (New York, 1927), I, 154.
17. The apparatus for study of *Titus Andronicus* is given in E. K. Chambers, *William Shakespeare* (Oxford, 1930), I, 312–22. A convenient summary of this material is that of A. M. Witherspoon (ed.), *Titus Andronicus*, "The Yale Shakespeare" (New Haven, 1926). I do not agree with Professor Witherspoon's description of the play; for Professor Witherspoon, though he has contributed notably to correcting theories of exclusively Senecan influences on Garnier (cf. Ch. II, note 36, *supra*), reverses himself with the much less Senecan English tragedy; in a selected list of twenty important studies of *Titus Andronicus*, he enters J. W. Cunliffe's *Influence of Seneca* with this comment: "An informative discussion of the major influence in *Titus* and kindred tragedies."
18. Cunliffe, *op. cit.*, p. 69.

19. *The Tragedie of Titus Andronicus*, ed. Charlotte Porter and Helen A. Clark (New York, 1903), p. 111.
20. *Confessio Amantis*, ed. Henry Morley (London, 1889), p. 288 (Bk. V "Avarice"; 7 "Violent Seizure").
21. And the dramatizing of horrors comes in part, of course, from the moral and mystery plays; cf. pp. 144 and 145 *infra*.
22. Gascoigne's *Works*, ed. Cunliffe, II, 181.
23. Cf. pp. 172 ff. *infra*.
24. The Belleforest Hamblet simply *shams* madness. Now, better than the conjecture that Kyd, the conjectured author of the lost *Ur-Hamlet*, combined the real madness of Hieronimo with the sham madness of Hamblet and thus made way for Shakespeare's Hamlet—better than this conjecture and more revealing is the actual disposition of Titus. For (?) Kyd's Hamblet may have leaned we know not how far in the one direction or the other. That Kyd in Hieronimo perfected the demeanor and language of madness, we know; that Titus (like Hamlet, I think) stands midway between shammed and semi-madness, is usually ignored: cf., e.g., J. M. Robertson, *The Problem of Hamlet* (London, 1919).

    I realize only too well that in calling the disposition of Hamlet ambiguous, I may seem to be indulging in critical ambiguity. What more I have to say, however, must await a later place; yet I hope that my general attack here is clear: we grasp or apprehend Hamlet as a whole, ambiguity and all, and only get into trouble when we try to fit him to an abstract, mental formula which would make him either sane or insane, either possessed completely of free will or not possessed of it. Unfortunately yes or no is seldom an adequate answer to the questions raised either by life or by art.
25. With this speech compare, and note the development in, Hotspur's threat "to dive into the bottom of the deep . . . and pluck up drowned honour by the locks." 1 *Hen.* IV, I, 3, 203 ff.
26. These stories do not account for one important situation, the lustful alliance between the Moor and Tamora; nor does any story very satisfactorily (Cf. Chambers, *William Shakespeare*). The alliance, however, in that it is a crude opposite of the Othello situation, seems by antithesis to anticipate the latter.
27. Cunliffe, *op. cit.*, p. 70.
28. *Metamorphoses*, ed. F. J. Miller (New York, 1928), VI, 520–1.
29. Cunliffe, *op. cit.*, pp. 69–70.

30. This is equivalent to ll. 508–10 in the Loeb edition, which reads *ornique*, line 509, for *ramique: Seneca's Tragedies*, ed. F. J. Miller (London, 1929), 2 vols.
31. T. S. Baynes came to the conclusion that some Seneca was read in the Stratford Grammar School; cf. "What Shakespeare Learnt at School," *Shakespeare Studies* (1894), 147. E. K. Chambers does not include Seneca, but, among other authors, "Ovid in abundance, Virgil, perhaps Horace or Terrence . . ." Cf. *William Shakespeare*, I, 10.
32. Cf. The Malone Society Reprint, ed. J. H. P. Pafford and W. W. Greg (Oxford, 1931).
33. See pp. 38 ff. *supra*.
34. The Malone Society Reprint, pp. 52–3.
35. *The Chester Plays*, ed. Hermann Deimling (E.E.T.S., 1893), pp. 63, 83, 99.
36. *Ibid.*, p. 99.
37. *Ancient Cornish Drama*, ed. Edwin Morris (Oxford, 1859); cf., e.g., I, 149 and 183.
38. "The Magi, Herod, and the Slaughter of the Innocents," in *Chief Pre-Shakespearean Dramas*, ed. J. Q. Adams (Boston, 1924), 158–66.
39. *York Mystery Plays*, ed. L. T. Smith (Oxford, 1885), Pageant XIX; cf. also XVI and XVII. Cf. *The Towneley Plays*, ed. A. W. Pollard (E.E.T.S., 1897), Pageant XIV and XVI.
40. I use an approximate date suggested by Courthope. E. K. Chambers says that the *Conflict of Conscience* "is strongly Protestant, and is probably much earlier than 1581"—that is, earlier than the first printed edition; cf. *The Elizabethan Stage* (Oxford, 1923).
41. L. E. Kastner and H. B. Charlton (eds.), *The Works of William Alexander* (S.T.S., 1921), I, clvii.
42. *The Fall of Princes*, Book IX, ed. Bergen, p. 990.
43. Cf. Farnham, *The Medieval Heritage of Elizabethan Tragedy* (Berkeley, Cal., 1936), p. 342.
44. See pp. 35–6 and 138 *supra*.

NOTES TO CHAPTER IV

TRANSFORMATIONS OF MEDIEVAL STRUCTURE: *Titus Andronicus* AND THE SHAKESPEAREAN PRACTICE

1. Professor Farnham's discussion of this general subject is of great interest; cf. *op. cit.*, pp. 432–37.

2. For the non-Senecan character of this speech and of the conception which lies behind it, see pp. 98 ff. and 115 *supra.*
3. The extraordinary attainment in *Romeo and Juliet* is beyond all doubt its tragic pitch. While tragic pitch depends on unfathomable quantities like Shakespeare's insights into people and their actions, yet it will be agreed I think that in this play it is primarily a poetic quality, one not confined to, but especially remarkable in, the "best" passages. It is a rhetorical quality, and consequently a few words about it are relevant to the present study.

In the universally admired passages the Petrarchism of the balcony-scene poetry is distinctly recognizable; and Malone identified the rhetorical affinities of Juliet's "marriage hymn" (II, 2, 1 ff.) with Barnaby Riche's *Farewell* and Marlowe's *Edward II.* Both the complicated traditions, folk and classical, and the exuberant imagination in the description of Queen Mab (I, 4, 53–95) have been effectively studied (cf., e.g., E. K. Chambers, *Midsummer Night's Dream* in the "Arden Shakespeare," Boston, 1916); and it is clear that dramatically the Queen Mab poetry functions as a contrast to Romeo's references to his ominous dream. Thus it is exactly parallel with what happens in *Titus Andronicus* II, 2, 1 ff. (cf. p. 136 *supra*), and also in the following passages. Doubtless the highest tragical intensity is contained in the lines of Romeo when he discovers the still form of Juliet in the monument, and the impelling imagery of this great passage is founded, as Steevens and Malone pointed out, on Daniel's *Complaint of Rosamond;* compare—

beauty's ensign yet
Is crimson in thy lips and in thy cheeks,
And death's pale flag is not advanced there.

Shall I believe
That unsubstantial Death is amorous,
And that the lean abhorred monster keeps
Thee here in dark to be his paramour?
(V, 3, 94–6; 102–5)

—this, with *Rosamond:*

When naught respecting death, the last of paines,
Plac'd his pale collours, th' ensigne of his might,
Vpon hys new-got spoyle before his right . . .

> Ah how me thinks I see death dallying seekes,
> To entertaine it selfe in loues sweet place:
> Decayed Roses of discoloured cheekes,
> Doe yet retaine deere notes of former grace:
> And ougly death sits faire within her face.
>
> (Ed. A. C. Sprague, ll. 605-7; 672-8)

Romeo's brilliant sad poetry contrasts with his optimistic lyricism at the beginning of the fifth act; and this contrast itself has been regarded as significantly comparable with Troilus' cheerfulness just before he receives evil news of Criseyde (cp. *R. & J.* V, 1-11 with Chaucer, *Troilus and Criseyde* V, 1164 ff.).

In comparison with such traditional elements as these in *Romeo and Juliet*, it may be mentioned that the Senecan critics have given some attention, for obvious reasons, to the Nurse. This is perfectly idle, for not only is the imprint of Elizabethan "realism" on her, but the whole conception of her rôle and personality springs from Brooke's poem.

4. A key to the mixed elements in the chronicle-history appears on the title page of a typical play (quarto, 1594):

> The First part of the Contention betwixt the two famous Houses of Yorke and Lancaster, with the death of the good Duke Humphrey: And the banishment and death of the Duke of Suffolke, and the Tragicall end of the proud Cardinall of Winchester, with the notable Rebellion of Iacke Cade: And the Duke of Yorkes first claime vnto the Crowne.

In other words contentions and rebellions are history, while the fall and death of a proud man is tragedy.

5. A. C. Bradley, *Shakespearean Tragedy* (London, 1932), p. 20.
6. Aristotle's *Poetics*, XI, 1, ed. S. H. Butcher (London, 1927), p. 41.
7. Gustav Freytag, *Technique of the Drama* (Chicago, 1895), p. 158.
8. I am speaking of the tragic and dramatic conception of *Richard III*, and am not forgetting the chronicles and the biography by (?) Sir Thomas More, which must have been themselves "tragical" narratives for Elizabethans. If, as Chambers conjectures (*William Shakespeare*, I, 303), the *Buckingham* said by Henslowe to have been played three times in January, 1594, is Shakespeare's *Richard III*, the confusion of the titles

could easily have followed from a popular association of Richard with Sackville's contribution to *The Mirror.*

9. Ed. A. C. Sprague, ll. 64–70.
10. T. S. Eliot, *Selected Essays* (New York, 1932), "Shakespeare and the Stoicism of Seneca" (1927), pp. 107–21. The sentence quoted is from p. 113.
11. *Ibid.*, p. 112.
12. *Ibid.*, p. 118.

NOTES TO CHAPTER V

Some Principles of Ethical Form in Pre-Shakespearean Tragic Literature

1. See p. 138 *supra.* Cf. Seneca's *De Clementia.*
2. Henry Peacham, *The Compleat Gentleman* (1634), ed. G. S. Gordon (Oxford, 1906).
3. Thomas Lodge, "To the Courteous Reader," prefatory to *The Workes of Lvcius Annaevs Seneca, Both Morrall and Naturall* (London, 1614).
4. Cf. pp. 210–11 *infra.*
5. Lodge, *op. cit.*, p. 741.
6. *Ibid.*, p. 732.
7. *An Apologie for Poetrie*, ed. Edward Arber (London, 1929), p. 45 and pp. 63 ff.
8. "It is a common practise now a daies amongst a sort of shifting companions, that runne through euery arte and thriue by none, to leaue the trade of *Nouerint* whereto they were borne, and busie themselues with the indeuors of Art, that could scarcelie latinize their necke-verse if they should haue neede; yet English *Seneca* read by candle light yeeldes manie good sentences, as *Bloud is a begger*, and so foorth: and if you intreate him faire in a frostie morning, he will affoord you whole *Hamlets*, I should say handfulls of tragical speaches. But ô griefe! *tempas edax rerum*, what's that will last alwaies? The sea exhaled by droppes will in continuance be drie, and *Seneca* let bloud line by line and page by page, at length must needes die to our stage: which makes his famisht followers to imitate the Kidde in *AEsop*, who enamored with the Foxes newfangles, forsooke all hopes of life to leape into a new occupation; and these men renowncing all possibilities of credit or estimation, to intermeddle with Italian translations: wherein how poorelie they haue plodded, (as those that are

neither prouenzall men, nor are able to distinguish of Articles,) let all indifferent Gentlemen that haue trauailed in that tongue, discerne by their twopenie pamphlets: and no meruaile though their home-born mediocritie be such in this matter; for what can be hoped of those, that thrust *Elisium* into hell, and haue not learned so long as they haue liued in the spheares, the iust measure of the Horizon without an hexameter. Sufficeth them to bodge vp a blanke verse with ifs and ands, and other while for recreation after their candle stuffe, hauing starched their beardes most curiouslie, to make a peripateticall path into the inner parts of the Citie, and spend two or three howers in turning ouer French *Doudie,* where they attract more infection in one minute, than they can do eloquence all dayes of their life, by conuersing with anie Authors of like argument." Thomas Nashe, "To the Gentlemen Students of both Vniuersities" (Summer, 1589), a preface to Robert Greene's *Menaphon,* ed. Edward Arber (London, 1880), pp. 9–10.

9. Farnham, *op. cit.*, pp. 101–2.
10. Since Professor Farnham's work has aided me importantly in framing the ideas contained in these pages, I should explain that my interpretation of this part of Boccaccio's morality is different from his. I do not find, as Professor Farnham does, a conception of responsibility in the conclusion of the *De Casibus;* this in itself is not very important, but I think that a demand on the part of Boccaccio for heroic activity in a semi-deterministic and unfavorable world, makes for tragedy of the first rank and is probably the key to the later Elizabethan attitude towards fate and free will.
11. Ed. Haslewood, II, 5.
12. I am thinking not only of the intrinsic merit of the poetry but also of it as background for *Romeo and Juliet.*
13. *Chief Pre-Shakespearean Dramas,* ed. J. Q. Adams (Boston, 1924), pp. 638–66.
14. *Early English Classical Tragedies,* ed. J. W. Cunliffe (Oxford, 1912), p. 292, l. 23.
15. Cf. p. 23 *supra.* Cf. L. B. Campbell, "Theories of Revenge in Renaissance England," *Mod. Philol.,* XXVIII (1931), 281–96.

INDEX

INDEX